VIBRATIONAL HEALING

Raising your Energy Frequency and Consciousness

Sarah Ripley

Vibrational Healing: Raising your Energy Frequency and Consciousness.

Copyright © 2024 Sarah Ripley & Street Cat Publishing

All rights reserved.

Other Titles by
Sarah Ripley:

Spirit Animals: Harnessing the Power of Spirit Guides and Their Messages

Sabbats and Esbats: A Modern Witch's Guide to Wiccan Rituals

Angel Numbers and Divine Numerology: Unlocking the Meaning and Divine Messages of the Universe

Conjure Your Desires: Rituals, Spells and Runes for Manifesting Your Dreams.

369 Manifesting your Dreams: A Manifestation Journal to Create the Life You Desire

The Shadow Work Journal: A Guide for Exploring your Hidden Self

The Power of the 369 Method: Unlock the Cosmic Code and Create the Life you Desire using the Law of Attraction

Join the Community to Receive Exclusive Bonus Content.

Scan the QR code to receive your FREE Self Care Affirmations!

Table of Contents

Vibrational Frequency

The human body is a symphony, not of sound, but of energy. Every cell, every organ, every system vibrates with a specific rhythm, contributing to the overall energy field that is us. Modern science tells us everything in the universe vibrates, from the tiniest atom to the farthest star, each at its own frequency. It stands to reason, then, that our bodies, composed of these very same vibrating particles, would do the same.

Imagine the universe as a vast symphony, with rhythms playing out on a grand scale. Seasonal changes ebb and flow like musical movements, and the tides rise and fall in a constant, rhythmic dance. But this symphony isn't just out there in the cosmos; it also resonates within us.

Our emotions aren't just fleeting feelings; vibrational healing proposes they have a physical counterpart – energy frequencies. Imagine each emotion resonating at a distinct pitch. Joy might vibrate at a high, clear frequency, while anger could be a lower, more discordant hum. These emotional frequencies are believed to interact with the symphony of vibrations occurring within our bodies.

Think of your body as a complex instrument, with each cell a tiny string vibrating at a specific rate. The collective hum of these cellular vibrations contributes to your overall energy field. According to this theory, our emotions can influence the vibrations within our cells. Strong negative emotions like anger or anxiety are believed to disrupt the harmony of these vibrations, potentially lowering your overall energy frequency. Conversely, positive emotions like joy or gratitude may promote a more balanced and higher frequency state.

This concept suggests a connection between vibrational frequency and well-being. A healthy body is believed to resonate within a specific frequency range. When your vibrational frequency drops due to negative emotions or other factors, it might impact your physical and emotional well-being. Conversely, practices that raise your vibrational frequency, like meditation or spending time in nature, could promote feelings of well-being and emotional balance.

This concept isn't merely theoretical. When we're stressed or overwhelmed, a shift occurs in our energy. Our breath quickens, muscles tense, and our overall energy plummets. Conversely, feelings of joy, peace, and love can have the opposite effect, leaving us feeling energized and light.

The idea of energy frequencies resonates with the intuitive notion that our physical and emotional states are intertwined. Just as a healthy body can influence a positive outlook, feeling happy and fulfilled can seem to energize us. This concept of vibrational frequency offers a framework for understanding this deeper connection, suggesting that our well-being is not just a physical matter, but an energetic one as well.

The mind and body are not isolated entities; they exist in a constant dance of influence. Researchers have long observed how our thoughts and behaviors can alter the body's rhythms. Anxious thoughts, for instance, trigger a cascade of stress hormones, prompting the heart rate to fluctuate erratically. Similarly, the sound vibrations of music have a demonstrable effect on our thoughts, emotions, and even our physiological systems.

This intricate interplay extends beyond the readily observable rhythms. Proponents of vibrational energy believe our thoughts and behaviors can also influence the subtler vibrations occurring at the cellular and even atomic levels. The theory suggests that by consciously altering our thoughts, behaviors, and even our surroundings, we can potentially modify these nanovibrations. These changes, in turn, are believed to ripple outward, impacting our mental and physical well-being in profound ways. This concept offers a fascinating perspective on the interconnectedness of mind, body, and the very fabric of our being.

The human body's symphony of energy can face a discordant note when cellular vibrations drop below a certain threshold. Science is beginning to explore the fascinating link between our physical state and the frequency at which our cells vibrate. Research suggests that a healthy human body resonates within a specific range, typically between 62-70 MHz. However, when this frequency dips below 62 MHz, cells can become susceptible to change and illness might take root.

For instance, a common cold or flu might be reflected in a cellular vibration around 58 MHz. The presence of fungal infections could further lower this frequency to 55 MHz. The numbers become even more concerning with conditions like Epstein-Barr virus, where the body's frequency is estimated to drop to 52 MHz. The most significant drop is associated with cancer, where cellular vibrations can plummet to 42 MHz or even lower. These correlations highlight the potential importance of maintaining a high cellular vibration for optimal health.

The good news is that we're not simply passive passengers in this energetic dance. There are steps we can take to raise our vibrational frequency and promote a sense of well-being. By understanding this connection between our energy and our health, we gain a new perspective on self-care, moving beyond just the physical aspects and embracing practices that nurture our energetic field as well.

This is where vibrational healing comes in. These practices aim to influence and elevate your energy frequency. The idea is that by using techniques like sound therapy, energy work, or even focusing on positive thoughts, you can promote a more harmonious state of vibration within your body. This, in turn, is believed to support emotional well-being and potentially contribute to better physical health.

Raising your Consciousness

Consciousness, that elusive spark of sentience that makes us distinctly human, has captivated philosophers and scientists for millennia. It's the wellspring of our thoughts, emotions, and perceptions, the essence of who we are. But what if there's more to this experience than just brain activity? Recent explorations in vibrational energy posit a fascinating connection. Here, we delve into how energy healing practices, believed to influence the body's subtle vibrations, might play a role in fostering a more awakened state of consciousness.

The path to a more awakened consciousness and energy healing share a common thread: a focus on addressing imbalances and fostering a sense of wholeness. Energy healing practices often target the flow of energy within the body, sometimes referred to as qi or life force. Proponents believe this energy is vital for both physical and emotional well-being, and that blockages or disruptions can hinder our overall state. By promoting a smooth flow of this energy, energy healing aims to create a foundation conducive to a more expansive consciousness.

Consider the role of self-awareness. Many energy healing modalities incorporate techniques like meditation and visualization, tools that enhance our ability to look inward. As we become more attuned to our subtle energy sensations and emotional states, we gain a deeper understanding of ourselves. This heightened self-awareness is a cornerstone of raising consciousness. By becoming more aware of our thoughts, emotions, and energy patterns, we gain greater control and can make conscious choices that align with our values and well-being.

Energy healing approaches health holistically, recognizing the interconnectedness of mind, body, and spirit. Raising consciousness, too, isn't merely about intellectual knowledge; it's about experiencing a sense of wholeness and alignment across all aspects of ourselves. Energy healing practices, by addressing imbalances on an energetic level, can contribute to this feeling of complete integration.

Finally, some energy healing practices cultivate a sense of intuition and connection to something larger than ourselves. This might involve connecting with the body's energy field, the natural world, or even a higher power. Raising consciousness often involves a similar expansion – a deepening sense of connection to the world around us and a heightened sense of intuition. Energy healing practices that foster these connections can contribute to an overall expansion of consciousness.

Many people find these practices to be valuable tools on their journey towards a more awakened state. By creating a foundation of well-being, self-awareness, and connection, energy healing can play a role in fostering a more expansive and integrated way of experiencing life, a central tenet of raising consciousness.

Assessing your Energy Frequency

Assessing your vibrational energy can be a fascinating journey of self-discovery. While there's no single scientific instrument to measure it definitively, several approaches can offer valuable insights.

Intuitive Methods:

Our bodies are like finely tuned instruments, constantly sending us messages through subtle cues. By becoming more attuned to these signals, we can gain valuable insights into our overall vibrational state. Imagine yourself radiating energy – when your vibration is high, it translates to a feeling of vitality and lightness. You move through your day with a spring in your step, a sense of ease that makes even mundane tasks feel effortless. It's like there's a wellspring of energy bubbling up from within, propelling you forward with a positive outlook.

On the other hand, a low vibrational state can manifest quite differently. You might find yourself feeling sluggish, weighed down by a fatigue that seeps into your bones. Aches and pains that weren't there before might crop up, and even simple movements feel like a chore. This is your body's way of signaling that your energetic reserves are depleted. By recognizing these cues, we can take steps to improve our vibrational state and return to a place of vibrancy and well-being.

Our emotional landscape also offers valuable clues about our vibrational state. When positive emotions like joy, gratitude, and peace become our natural way of being, it's a strong indicator that we're vibrating at a higher frequency. These emotions aren't fleeting bursts of happiness, but a more constant undercurrent that colors our interactions with the world. They radiate outward, creating a magnetic field that attracts positive experiences and like-minded people. It's as if we're operating on the same energetic wavelength, fostering a sense of connection and ease.

Conversely, if negativity becomes our default setting, with anger, fear, or frustration constantly bubbling up, it suggests a dip in our vibrational frequency. These emotions act like energetic cobwebs, weighing us down and creating a dissonance with the positive flow of the universe. It can feel like we're pushing against a current, making it harder to attract what we desire. By becoming more aware of our emotional patterns, we can identify areas that need attention and work towards cultivating a more positive emotional state. This shift will naturally elevate our vibration and open us up to a more harmonious and fulfilling experience of life.

The clarity of our mind also acts as a beacon for our vibrational state. When our thoughts are sharp and focused, existing in the present moment rather than dwelling on the past or fretting about the future, we can navigate life's challenges with greater ease. This inner peace and focus allows us to tap into our intuition, that wellspring of wisdom that resides within. It's like having a built-in compass, guiding us towards the right choices and opportunities. This sense of mental coherence is a strong indication that we're vibrating at a higher frequency.

By cultivating mindfulness, we become more attuned to the subtle whispers from our body, mind, and emotions. These whispers, when acknowledged, provide valuable insights into our current energetic state. Imagine yourself as a radio – if you're tuned into a clear frequency, the music comes through crisp and vibrant. However, a mismatched frequency results in static and distortion. Similarly, a high vibration allows us to experience life with clarity and fullness, while a lower vibration can create a sense of muddled confusion. By paying attention to these internal cues, we can fine-tune our energetic dial and step into a more harmonious and fulfilling way of being.

Biofeedback:

While intuitive methods like body awareness and emotional state are incredibly powerful tools for gauging your vibration, there are additional approaches that offer more indirect clues. For those seeking a more scientific approach, biofeedback machines can be a fascinating option. These devices act as a window into your body's internal workings, monitoring physiological responses like heart rate and respiration. Because these responses are often closely linked to your emotional state, biofeedback can provide valuable insights into your overall energy level. Imagine biofeedback as a translator, deciphering the language of your body and presenting it in a clear, data-driven way.

This information isn't just for passive observation. Biofeedback can also be used as a training tool. By receiving real-time feedback on your physiological state, you can learn to regulate your emotions and potentially raise your vibration. It's like having a personal energetic coach, guiding you towards a more balanced and optimal state. Through biofeedback, you can learn to calm your mind during moments of stress, fostering a sense of inner peace that naturally elevates your vibration. While biofeedback offers a unique perspective, it's important to remember that it complements, rather than replaces, the intuitive methods we've explored previously. By combining these approaches, you gain a comprehensive understanding of your energetic landscape, empowering you to cultivate a life that vibrates with positivity and well-being.

Muscle Testing:

Similar to biofeedback machines, muscle testing provides a way to receive indirect clues about your energetic state. By focusing on specific questions and observing the muscular response, a practitioner can help you identify areas of energy depletion or stagnation. The theory goes that the strength or weakness of your muscular response acts as an indicator of your energy's flow and quality. For instance, a strong muscle response might suggest your energy is flowing freely in that area, while a weak response could indicate a blockage or imbalance.

For muscle testing, it's recommended to seek out a practitioner trained in this specific technique. Look for someone with a good reputation and experience in energetic healing modalities.

During your session, the practitioner will likely ask you to focus on a question related to your energy. This could be a general inquiry like "Is my overall vibration high right now?" or something more specific like "Is there an energy blockage affecting my creativity?"

The actual test involves the practitioner gently applying pressure to a designated muscle, often the deltoid in the arm, but it can vary. While holding this position, you'll be asked to answer "yes" or "no" to your question while maintaining your focus on it.

The interpretation of the response hinges on the strength or weakness of your muscle response. A strong response is generally seen as an indicator of free-flowing energy, while a weak response could suggest a blockage or imbalance in your energetic system.

This information can then be used to develop a personalized plan to address these imbalances and promote a more harmonious flow of energy throughout your body.

Dowsing with a Pendulum:

Dowsing offers another avenue for those seeking to understand their energy levels. This practice utilizes a pendulum or similar tool, acting as a bridge between your intuition and the energetic world. By asking focused yes or no questions related to your vibrational state, the movement of the pendulum provides a form of energetic feedback. Many find dowsing to be a deeply intuitive tool, one that resonates with their inner knowing and offers valuable insights that traditional methods might miss. Imagine the pendulum as a compass needle, subtly responding to the energetic shifts within your body.

First, find a pendulum that feels comfortable in your hand. It can be a crystal pendant, a weight on a string, or any balanced object. Then, create a calm and quiet space where you can relax and focus. Take a moment to clear your pendulum, visualizing white light washing over it to cleanse any lingering energy.

The next step is to establish a communication system with your pendulum. Decide on a specific movement to represent "yes" (like a clockwise circle) and another for "no" (counter-clockwise perhaps). You can also use back-and-forth swings for "yes" and stillness for "no." Hold the pendulum still and concentrate on your chosen "yes" answer, then ask aloud "is this your yes response?" Observe the movement and repeat for "no" to program your pendulum.

Begin with some grounding questions you know the answer to, like "is my name [your name]?" This gets you comfortable with the pendulum's movements and builds trust. Once you feel comfortable, move on to questions about your energy levels. Phrase them clearly and concisely, for example "Is my vibration high right now?" or "Do I need to take steps to improve my energy flow?"

As you ask your questions, observe the pendulum's movement based on your established yes/no responses. Trust your intuition and don't get caught up in overthinking the answer. When your session is complete, thank your pendulum and clear it again with the white light visualization.

Remember, dowsing is a personal practice. There may be days when the pendulum doesn't give a clear response. Be patient, experiment, and see if it resonates with you. If the pendulum isn't moving clearly, take it as a sign to revisit the practice at another time.

The effectiveness of dowsing is a personal experience. Some find it to be a powerful tool for self-discovery, while others may not resonate with its practice. Regardless of your initial stance, there's value in approaching dowsing with an open mind. By experimenting with this technique and asking questions about your energy levels, you might uncover hidden patterns or imbalances. This newfound awareness can empower you to take action and implement practices that elevate your vibration and cultivate a sense of overall well-being.

Understanding your body's energetic state is just the first step on a path to greater well-being. By tuning into your emotions, physical sensations, and mental clarity, you can gain valuable insights into your vibrational frequency.

Now that we've explored how to identify your energetic baseline, let's delve into the world of vibrational healing techniques! We'll explore a range of practices like chakra clearing, Ayurveda, and sound therapy, all of which aim to promote a more harmonious flow of energy within your body. These techniques are believed to influence your vibrational frequency, leading to a more balanced and awakened state of being.

Sound Therapy

Sound therapy has emerged as a fascinating tool in the realm of vibrational healing. It's based on the principle that sound waves and vibrations can interact with our bodies on a cellular level, potentially influencing our energy frequency and overall well-being.

Imagine your body as a complex instrument, with each cell vibrating at a specific rate. Sound therapy introduces specific sound waves that some believe can resonate with these cellular vibrations. In a state of disharmony, these vibrations might be chaotic or sluggish. Sound therapy aims to introduce harmonious frequencies that can help retune these cellular vibrations, creating a more balanced and orderly state within the body.

The world of sound therapy offers a diverse toolbox of instruments, each with its own unique properties. Tuning forks, for instance, transform from a musician's tool into a targeted instrument for energetic balance. Practitioners believe that when struck, these specially crafted forks emit specific sonic frequencies that resonate with different parts of the body. Like tiny tuning keys, they can adjust imbalances within the body's energetic field.

The key lies in the specific frequencies each tuning fork produces. By carefully selecting forks based on their frequency, practitioners can target a variety of issues. Lower frequencies, with their long, soothing waves, are often used to promote relaxation and ease pain. Imagine them as gentle waves lapping at the shore, calming a restless mind and easing tension in muscles. Conversely, higher frequencies, with their shorter, more stimulating waves, might be used to invigorate stagnant energy or reduce inflammation. They act like a burst of sunshine, activating sluggish areas and promoting cellular repair.

Here's a list with some commonly cited frequencies and their benefits:

- **174 Hz** - This low frequency is thought to promote relaxation, pain relief, and a sense of security.
- **285 Hz** - This frequency is believed to stimulate tissue and organ repair and promote feelings of safety and well-being.
- **396 Hz** - This mid-range frequency is associated with releasing fear, guilt, and negativity, promoting a sense of forgiveness and self-love.
- **417 Hz** - This frequency is said to facilitate positive change and transformation, potentially aiding in overcoming past trauma.
- **528 Hz** - Often referred to as the "love frequency" or "miracle tone," this frequency is believed to promote healing, creativity, and intuition.
- **639 Hz** - This frequency is thought to improve communication, relationships, and feelings of harmony.
- **741 Hz** - This high frequency is associated with enhanced intuition, self-expression, and problem-solving abilities.

- **Solfeggio Frequencies** - These six tones (396 Hz, 417 Hz, 528 Hz, 639 Hz, 741 Hz, and 852 Hz) are derived from ancient musical scales and are believed to have specific healing properties.

This targeted approach allows practitioners to address a wide range of concerns. Muscle tension that disrupts your freedom of movement might be soothed by the vibrations of a tuning fork placed on a specific trigger point. Headaches, often rooted in congested energy pathways, could be eased by placing the fork on acupressure points, believed to be gateways along the body's energetic meridians. The sound waves themselves are thought to interact with the body's tissues on a cellular level, influencing everything from blood flow and muscle tension to the release of endorphins, the body's natural painkillers.

By incorporating tuning forks into a sound therapy session, practitioners create a unique soundscape that goes beyond the physical realm. The carefully chosen frequencies not only target physical imbalances but can also have a profound effect on our emotional well-being. The deep hum of a low-frequency fork can lull us into a state of peace, while the brighter tones of a higher-frequency fork might spark feelings of clarity and focus. In this way, tuning forks become instruments of holistic healing, addressing both the physical and emotional aspects of our being, promoting a sense of harmony and well-being that resonates from the inside out.

Stepping into the realm of sound therapy, we encounter another fascinating instrument – the singing bowl. Renowned for their deep, resonant tones, these bowls aren't just beautiful objects; they are powerful tools for vibrational healing. When struck or played around the rim, singing bowls vibrate, creating rich sound waves that wash over the body. Imagine these waves as a gentle massage for your energetic field, dissolving tension and promoting a sense of calm.

The magic lies in the specific frequencies produced by each singing bowl. Different sizes and materials create unique tonal variations, allowing practitioners to tailor the sound experience to the specific needs of the individual. Deep, booming tones, often produced by larger bowls, are known for their deeply relaxing properties. They lull the nervous system into a state of tranquility, much like the rhythmic crash of ocean waves easing anxieties. These lower frequencies can also promote the release of muscle tension, allowing the body to unwind and release pent-up stress.

The immersive experience of sound waves created by singing bowls extends beyond physical relaxation. As the waves envelop you, they can have a profound effect on the mind. The repetitive nature of the sound acts as a gentle lull, quieting the chatter of the mind and promoting a state of focused meditation. In this quieter space, worries and anxieties begin to lose their hold, replaced by a sense of inner peace and clarity. This mindful state can be a catalyst for deeper self-awareness, allowing you to connect with your intuition and identify areas where your energy might be stagnant or depleted.

But the benefits of singing bowls extend even further. In this state of tranquility, the body's natural healing mechanisms are believed to be amplified. The deep vibrations are thought to stimulate cellular regeneration and improve circulation, promoting an overall sense of well-being. Singing bowls become instruments of holistic healing, addressing the physical, mental, and emotional aspects of our being. By creating a resonant soundscape, they help us vibrate at a higher frequency, promoting a sense of harmony and well-being that resonates from the inside out.

In the symphony of sound therapy instruments, gongs, drums, and chimes can also play a distinct role, offering a unique range of benefits.

Gongs are the titans of sound therapy, renowned for their powerful vibrations that resonate throughout the entire body. When struck, these large metallic discs produce a complex wave of sound that seems to envelop the listener. This immersive experience can be deeply transformative. The initial attack of the gong's sound can be startling, but it quickly gives way to a cascade of overtones and harmonics that wash over the body, releasing blockages and promoting a sense of deep relaxation. Imagine the gong's sound as a sonic wave that travels not just through your ears, but through every cell in your being, dislodging stagnant energy and promoting a profound sense of renewal.

The gong's power lies not just in its volume, but also in its ability to create a binaural beat effect. This occurs when the gong produces two slightly different frequencies that stimulate the brainwave patterns. These altered brainwaves can induce a deeply meditative state, promoting feelings of peace and inner calm. Additionally, the gong's vibrations are believed to help clear energetic imbalances, allowing your body's natural healing mechanisms to function more effectively.

Drums, with their primal pulse, bring a different energy to sound therapy sessions. The rhythmic beats resonate with the body's natural heartbeat, grounding us and fostering a sense of connection. Unlike the expansive sound of the gong, drums provide a focused energy that can stimulate stagnant energy flow or promote emotional release. Faster drum rhythms can be invigorating, encouraging movement and a sense of vitality. Slower, more deliberate beats can create a safe space for emotional processing, allowing pent-up feelings to surface and be released.

The type of drum used also plays a role. Handpans, with their ethereal sounds, can create a sense of serenity, while frame drums, with their sharp attacks, can be more stimulating. By incorporating different drums into a session, practitioners can create a dynamic soundscape that caters to a variety of needs.

Chimes, with their soft, melodic tinkling, offer a more subtle approach to sound therapy. Unlike the powerful gongs or the rhythmic drums, chimes provide a gentle, calming influence. The cascading notes can lull the mind into a meditative state, promoting feelings of peace and tranquility. Imagine chimes as a soothing balm for the nervous system, washing away stress and anxiety with each delicate peal.

Chimes can also be used to clear stagnant energy. The high-pitched tones are believed to have a cleansing effect, helping to remove blockages and promote a smoother flow of energy throughout the body. Additionally, the specific arrangements of chimes, tuned to particular scales, can create specific energetic resonances that can target emotional or physical imbalances.

By incorporating gongs, drums, and chimes into a sound therapy session, practitioners create a rich tapestry of sound that can address a wide range of needs. From the deep, transformative power of the gong to the grounding rhythm of the drum and the gentle whispers of the chimes, each instrument plays a vital role in promoting a sense of harmony and well-being.

The world of sound therapy extends far beyond the handcrafted instruments specifically designed for this purpose. Our very world vibrates with a symphony of sounds, each with the potential to influence our well-being. Take music, for instance – it transcends mere entertainment to become a powerful tool for influencing our vibrational state. Carefully crafted pieces composed with specific frequencies in mind can create a deeply immersive experience that resonates on a cellular level. Imagine uplifting melodies acting like sunshine for your soul, energizing and igniting your creative spark. Conversely, calming compositions can lull you into a state of tranquility, like gentle waves lapping at the shore, washing away stress and promoting deep relaxation.

This inherent power of music is precisely why music therapy has become a recognized field. Trained professionals utilize music to address a wide range of physical, emotional, and cognitive conditions. Upbeat tempos and stimulating rhythms can be incorporated to improve motor skills in stroke patients or enhance cognitive function in those with dementia. Conversely, soothing melodies and calming harmonies can be used to manage anxiety, promote relaxation in cancer patients, or even ease pain during childbirth. Music therapy recognizes the profound connection between our auditory system and our emotional state. By carefully selecting music and incorporating it into a therapeutic setting, music therapists create a soundscape that can evoke specific emotions and physiological responses, promoting healing and a sense of well-being.

The therapeutic potential of sound extends far beyond the realm of musical compositions. Our world is a constant soundscape, filled with natural acoustics that hold a surprising power to influence our emotional state. Take a walk on a beach, for instance. The rhythmic crash of ocean waves isn't just a pleasant backdrop; it's a symphony of deep, low-frequency sounds. These low tones have a demonstrably calming effect, promoting the release of stress hormones and lowering blood pressure. Imagine them as a soothing balm for your nervous system, washing away tension with each rhythmic boom.

Similarly, the gentle rustling of leaves in the wind or the cascading melody of a babbling brook offer a different kind of sonic therapy. These lighter, high-frequency sounds act more like a gentle breeze, promoting feelings of peace and tranquility. They can lull the mind into a state of mindfulness, allowing worries to melt away and replaced by a sense of serenity. This connection to nature's sounds goes beyond a simple auditory experience. Studies have shown that spending time immersed in natural environments can demonstrably boost our immune system function. Immersing yourself in a forest bathed in sunlight, the sounds of birdsong filling the air, allows you to reconnect with the earth's natural frequencies. This reconnection is believed to have a grounding effect, fostering a sense of belonging and promoting overall well-being.

Nature's symphony offers a powerful reminder that sound therapy isn't just about using external instruments to create specific vibrations. It's about cultivating a deeper awareness of the world around us and harnessing the inherent vibratory power of the universe. By taking a moment to truly listen to the sounds of nature, we can tap into a source of healing and harmony that has existed for millennia. Whether it's the rhythmic crash of waves, the rustling of leaves, or the gurgle of a stream, these natural soundscapes hold the key to unlocking a sense of peace, grounding, and a renewed connection to the world around us.

Chakra Clearing and Balancing

Chakra clearing or balancing dives into the fascinating world of subtle energy within the body. Our bodies have seven main energy centers, called chakras, each linked to specific organs, emotions, and aspects of consciousness. Imagine these chakras as swirling vortexes of energy, and their balanced flow is said to be vital for overall well-being.

The blockages or imbalances within these chakras can disrupt the smooth flow of energy, potentially leading to physical or emotional issues. Chakra clearing practices aim to address these imbalances and restore a harmonious flow of energy throughout the body.

This concept connects to vibrational healing in a unique way. Think of each chakra as a vibrant energy center, pulsating at a specific frequency. When a chakra is balanced and clear, it's believed to vibrate at its optimal frequency, contributing to a healthy overall energy state. Conversely, a blocked or imbalanced chakra might vibrate at a disharmonious frequency, potentially disrupting your overall vibrational energy.

Chakra clearing practices aim to remove blockages and restore a balanced flow of energy within each chakra. By addressing these imbalances, these practices are believed to promote a more harmonious symphony of vibrations throughout your body. This, in turn, could contribute to a higher overall vibrational frequency.

Many people find chakra clearing practices to be helpful for managing stress, promoting relaxation, and fostering a sense of inner balance. By creating a more balanced and relaxed state, these practices create an environment conducive to raising your vibrational frequency.

These chakras, visualized as swirling vortices of energy, are believed to be aligned along the spine, starting at the base and rising to the crown of the head. As energy flows freely through these centers, we experience a sense of balance and vitality. Conversely, blockages or imbalances within these chakras can manifest as physical or emotional disharmony. Each chakra is associated with a specific color, element, and set of characteristics.

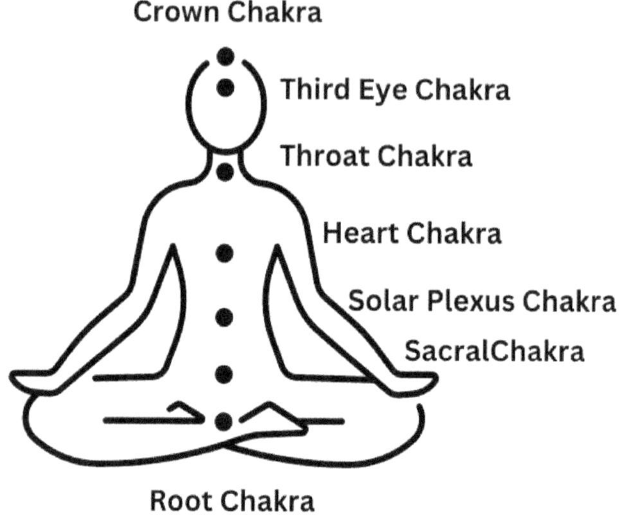

- **Root Chakra (Muladhara):**
    - Location: Base of the spine
    - Color: Red
    - Element: Earth
    - Represents: Security, stability, grounding

- **Sacral Chakra (Svadhisthana):**
    - Location: Lower abdomen
    - Color: Orange
    - Element: Water
    - Represents: Creativity, sensuality, emotions

- **Solar Plexus Chakra (Manipura):**
  - Location: Upper abdomen
  - Color: Yellow
  - Element: Fire
  - Represents: Personal power, willpower, confidence

- **Heart Chakra (Anahata):**
  - Location: Center of the chest
  - Color: Green
  - Element: Air
  - Represents: Love, compassion, empathy

- **Throat Chakra (Vishuddha):**
  - Location: Throat
  - Color: Blue
  - Element: Sound
  - Represents: Communication, self-expression, truth

- **Third Eye Chakra (Ajna):**
  - Location: Brow point
  - Color: Indigo
  - Element: Light
  - Represents: Intuition, wisdom, insight

- **Crown Chakra (Sahasrara):**
  - Location: Top of the head
  - Color: Violet
  - Element: Spirit
  - Represents: Spirituality,

consciousness, connection to the divine

The **Root Chakra**, also known as Muladhara in Sanskrit, is the foundation of our energetic body. Located at the base of the spine, it's symbolically linked to the earth element. Imagine it as the energetic root that tethers us to the physical world, providing a sense of stability, security, and grounding. When the Root Chakra is balanced, we feel safe, supported, and confident in our ability to navigate life's challenges.

This chakra is all about our basic needs and sense of survival. It governs our primal instincts, our fight-or-flight response, and our connection to the physical world. A balanced Root Chakra allows us to feel a sense of belonging, whether it's to our family, community, or simply the planet itself. It fosters feelings of safety and security, allowing us to relax and trust that our needs will be met.

However, an imbalanced Root Chakra can manifest in various ways. Feelings of insecurity, fear of the unknown, and a constant state of fight-or-flight can be signs that your Root Chakra is out of whack. Physical manifestations might include chronic lower back pain, constipation, or issues with the immune system.

The good news is that there are ways to bring your Root Chakra back into balance. Immersing yourself in nature is a powerful first step. The earth element, the energetic foundation of the

Root Chakra, has a natural ability to restore our sense of grounding. Take a walk barefoot on the earth, feeling the cool grass or warm sand beneath your feet. Imagine this connection as an energetic circuit, drawing stability and security from the very ground you walk on. Activities that connect you to your basic needs can also be nurturing. Perhaps it's spending time in your own garden, tending to your plants and witnessing their growth, a metaphor for your own resilience. Cooking a nourishing meal from scratch, the act of preparing and consuming food, can be a grounding ritual that connects you to your primal need for sustenance.

Yoga postures, known as asanas, offer another avenue for balancing the Root Chakra. Specific poses that target the base of the spine and pelvic floor are particularly beneficial. Mountain Pose (Tadasana) might seem simple, but standing tall with a rooted stance cultivates a sense of inner strength and connection to the earth. Warrior poses, Virabhadrasana I and II, encourage stability and confidence, while Child's Pose (Balasana) provides a safe haven for deep relaxation and inner reflection. These postures, when practiced mindfully, can help release blockages and promote the flow of energy within the Root Chakra.

The world of crystals can also play a supporting role. Crystals with grounding properties, like red jasper or hematite, are believed to vibrate at specific frequencies that resonate with the Root Chakra. Holding these stones during meditation or simply keeping them nearby can be a subtle reminder to focus on your sense of security and stability. The act of consciously choosing these grounding crystals and incorporating them into your self-care practices can become a ritual in itself, reinforcing your intention to cultivate a balanced Root Chakra.

By nurturing your Root Chakra, you cultivate a strong foundation for your entire energetic system. A balanced Root Chakra allows you to feel safe, supported, and empowered to take on the world with confidence. It's the energetic starting point from which all other chakras can flourish.

The **Sacral Chakra**, also known as Svadhisthana in Sanskrit, is our center of creativity, sensuality, and emotional expression. Located just below the navel, it's associated with the water element, symbolizing fluidity, connection, and our capacity to go with the flow. Imagine it as a wellspring of creative energy, constantly bubbling forth with ideas, desires, and a zest for life. When the Sacral Chakra is balanced, we feel vibrant, passionate, and in touch with our deepest emotions. We can express ourselves authentically and embrace healthy relationships.

On an energetic level, the Sacral Chakra vibrates at a specific frequency, influencing how we experience and interact with the world. A balanced frequency allows for a healthy flow of energy, fostering a sense of abundance and pleasure. This energy can manifest as creativity in the arts, but it can also extend to our capacity for intimacy and connection. A strong Sacral Chakra allows us to navigate emotional waters with grace, expressing our feelings openly and honestly.

However, a blocked or imbalanced Sacral Chakra can cause a variety of issues. Creative stagnation, a lack of motivation, and difficulty with emotional expression can all be signs that your Sacral Chakra needs attention. You might find yourself clinging to unhealthy relationships or struggling to embrace new experiences. Physical manifestations could include lower back pain, reproductive issues, or even a general lack of vitality.

There are a multitude of ways to retune the frequency of your Sacral Chakra and restore its vibrant energy flow. Rekindling your creativity is a powerful first step. Activities that ignite your imagination, like dancing, painting, or writing, can be like pressing the reset button on your creative wellspring. Let loose, embrace experimentation, and allow yourself to be guided by the inherent creative energy that flows through you. Don't be afraid to explore new mediums or revisit old hobbies – the key is to find activities that spark joy and a sense of self-expression.

Immersing yourself in nature, particularly near bodies of water like oceans or lakes, can also work wonders for your Sacral Chakra. The water element, the very essence of this chakra, has a natural ability to revitalize and promote emotional fluidity. Imagine the sound of waves gently lapping at the shore as a sonic massage, washing away stagnation and emotional blockages. Feel the cool water on your skin, a physical reminder of the cleansing and transformative power of this element. Simply sitting by a lake or strolling along a beach, breathing in the fresh air and allowing the rhythmic sounds of nature to wash over you, can create a sense of deep peace and emotional equilibrium.

Yoga postures that target the hips and lower abdomen are another valuable tool for balancing the Sacral Chakra. As with the Root Chakra, mindful movement and a focus on the breath are key. Specific poses like Cobra Pose (Bhujangasana) can help open up the hips and lower back, promoting a healthy flow of energy. Hip circles and gentle twists can also be beneficial, encouraging flexibility and releasing any tension that might be hindering your creative flow. Remember, these postures aren't about achieving perfect form; it's about moving your body with intention and awareness, allowing your breath to guide your movements and gently releasing any energetic blockages. By incorporating these practices into your life, you become an active participant in nurturing your Sacral Chakra. As you cultivate a vibrant and balanced flow of energy within this chakra, you'll witness a blossoming of your creativity, sensuality, and emotional expression, allowing you to experience life with passion and authenticity.

The **Solar Plexus Chakra**, also known as Manipura in Sanskrit, sits like a radiant sun at the center of your upper abdomen. It's the powerhouse of your energetic system, governing your sense of personal power, willpower, and self-confidence. Imagine it as a burning ember, radiating warmth and vitality throughout your being. When your Solar Plexus Chakra is balanced, you feel confident, assertive, and capable of achieving your goals. You possess a healthy sense of self-worth and radiate a powerful energy that allows you to step into the world with purpose.

On an energetic level, the Solar Plexus Chakra vibrates at a specific frequency, influencing your sense of inner strength and motivation. A balanced frequency promotes a healthy flow of energy, fostering feelings of confidence, decisiveness, and a drive to succeed. This energy isn't about arrogance or dominance; it's about a deep sense of self-belief and the willpower to turn your dreams into reality. It's the fire in your belly that propels you forward, allowing you to overcome challenges and chase your ambitions.

However, an imbalanced Solar Plexus Chakra can manifest in a variety of ways. Feelings of self-doubt, low self-esteem, and a lack of motivation can all be signs that your inner fire needs tending. You might find yourself constantly seeking external validation or struggling to make decisions. Physically, digestive issues, blood sugar imbalances, or even chronic fatigue can be associated with a blocked Solar Plexus Chakra.

There are a multitude of ways to stoke the flames of your Solar Plexus Chakra and reignite your inner fire. Stepping outside your comfort zone is a potent strategy. Public speaking, even if the thought makes your palms sweat, can be a powerful way to challenge yourself and build confidence. Imagine the initial fear transforming into a surge of empowerment as you effectively communicate your ideas. Taking on a leadership role, even in a small way, can also be invigorating. Volunteer for a project at work, or take charge of organizing a social event with friends. As you navigate the challenges and see your efforts come to fruition, your self-belief will naturally start to soar. Don't be afraid to explore new hobbies that spark your excitement. Whether it's learning a new language, picking up a paintbrush, or enrolling in a dance class, activities that ignite your passion will inherently boost your sense of self-worth.

Spending time in sunshine isn't just about enjoying a warm day; it's about harnessing the natural fire energy of the sun to energize your Solar Plexus Chakra. Imagine basking in the sun's warmth, feeling its golden rays penetrate your skin and seep deep into your core. This isn't just a passive experience; visualize the sunlight actively stimulating your Solar Plexus Chakra, infusing it with vibrant energy. As you soak up the sun's rays, take a few deep breaths, allowing the invigorating energy to course through your entire being.

Certain yoga postures that target the core and strengthen the abdominal muscles are also believed to be stimulating for the Solar Plexus Chakra. Boat Pose (Navasana) or Warrior III (Virabhadrasana III) require core engagement, which translates to building inner strength and willpower. Remember, these postures aren't just about achieving a perfect pose; it's about the mindful movement and the connection with your breath. As you hold these postures, focus on the sensations in your body and feel your core muscles activate. Imagine this activation as a spark igniting the fire within your Solar Plexus Chakra. With each inhale, draw in invigorating energy, and with each exhale, release any doubts or anxieties that might be holding you back. By incorporating these practices into your life, you become an active participant in cultivating a strong and vibrant Solar Plexus Chakra. As your inner fire burns brightly, you'll radiate confidence, self-belief, and the unwavering determination to turn your dreams into reality.

The **heart chakra**, also known as Anahata in Sanskrit, lies at the center of your chest, acting as a bridge between your lower chakras, focused on material existence, and your higher chakras, connected to spirituality. It's here where the energy of love, compassion, and empathy resides. When your heart chakra is balanced and vibrating at a high frequency, you experience a deep sense of love and connection, not just for others but also for yourself. This love radiates outwards, fostering positive relationships and attracting like-minded souls.

The energy of the heart chakra resonates with specific frequencies, some believe tones around 528Hz or 639Hz can promote feelings of love and forgiveness. These frequencies can be found in certain types of music or sound therapy sessions designed to activate and balance the heart chakra. By incorporating these frequencies into your life, you might find it easier to cultivate feelings of compassion and understanding.

However, a blocked or imbalanced heart chakra can manifest in a variety of ways. You might find yourself struggling to forgive, feeling closed off to love, or experiencing difficulty connecting with others on a deeper level. A sense of isolation and loneliness can take root. By nurturing your heart chakra through practices like meditation, acts of kindness, or spending time in nature, you can restore its balance and allow its energy to flow freely. This, in turn, allows you to experience the profound joy, compassion, and connection that this vital chakra has to offer.

There are many ways to clear and balance your heart chakra, allowing its energy to flow freely and radiate outward. One approach is through self-compassion and forgiveness. Holding onto anger, resentment, or past hurts can create blockages in the heart chakra. Taking time to forgive yourself and others, even for seemingly small transgressions, can help to release this pent-up energy. Practices like journaling or meditation can be helpful tools for facilitating forgiveness and self-love.

Connecting with nature is another powerful way to nurture your heart chakra. Immersing yourself in the beauty of the natural world, feeling the sun on your skin or the earth beneath your feet, can have a profound grounding effect. The vibrant colors of flowers or the calming rhythm of waves can promote feelings of peace and connection. Spending time in nature allows you to step outside the daily grind and reconnect with the simple joys of being alive.

Acts of kindness, big or small, can also play a significant role in balancing your heart chakra. Opening your heart to others through volunteering, helping a friend in need, or simply offering a smile to a stranger allows you to experience the joy of giving and fosters a sense of connection to the world around you. These acts of kindness not only benefit the recipient but also generate a positive feedback loop, nurturing your own sense of compassion and well-being.

Finally, incorporating practices that focus on the heart chakra itself can be very beneficial. Meditation focused on feelings of love and compassion, or yoga postures that open the chest area, can all help to stimulate and balance the heart chakra's energy. By incorporating these practices into your routine, you can create a foundation for a more open and loving heart, allowing you to experience the full potential of this vital energy center.

The **throat chakra**, Vishuddha in Sanskrit, resides at your throat, acting as the bridge between your thoughts and your voice. It governs communication, self-expression, and your ability to speak your truth. When this chakra is balanced and its energy vibrates at a high frequency, your voice is clear and confident. You express yourself authentically and with ease, and you're able to listen openly to others. This creates a space for genuine connection and fosters healthy relationships.

Vishuddha is believed to resonate with the color

blue and the element of sound. Some frequencies around 528Hz are thought to be particularly beneficial for this chakra, promoting clear communication and creative expression. Certain chants or mantras that incorporate these frequencies can be used to activate and balance the throat chakra.

However, a blocked throat chakra can manifest in a variety of ways. You might find yourself struggling to express yourself clearly, or you might hold back from speaking your truth for fear of judgment. Feeling unheard or misunderstood by others can also be a sign of an imbalance. This can lead to frustration, isolation, and difficulty building strong relationships.

There are many ways to clear and balance your throat chakra, allowing your voice to flow freely and your truth to be heard. One approach is through honest self-expression. Journaling, talking to a trusted friend, or even expressing yourself creatively through art or music can help to release pent-up emotions and allow your voice to be heard, even if it's just by yourself initially.

Singing is another powerful tool for balancing the throat chakra. The act of using your voice freely, whether through singing along to your favorite tunes or joining a choir, can help to loosen blockages and strengthen the flow of energy in this area. Even humming or chanting simple mantras can be beneficial.

Finally, practices that focus on mindful communication can be very helpful. This means actively listening to others and expressing yourself with clarity and honesty. By being present in conversations and avoiding interrupting or speaking over others, you demonstrate respect and create a space for genuine connection. This mindful communication not only benefits your relationships but also strengthens the energy flow within your throat chakra, allowing you to speak your truth with confidence and clarity.

The **third eye chakra**, Ajna in Sanskrit, rests between your brows, acting as the gateway to your intuition, wisdom, and insight. It's the seat of your sixth sense, where your perception transcends the physical world and connects with a deeper well of knowing. Imagine it as a cosmic antenna, finely tuned to pick up subtle energetic frequencies and translate them into intuitive whispers. When your third eye chakra is balanced and its energy vibrates at a high frequency, your intuition becomes a sharp and reliable guide. You gain a clear vision for your life's path, not just the immediate steps in front of you, but the overarching direction that aligns with your soul's purpose. This awakened state allows you to see through illusions and discern the underlying truth of a situation. You can navigate challenges with grace, make decisions with unwavering confidence, and tap into a wellspring of creative inspiration.

A blocked third eye chakra, however, can manifest in a multitude of ways. You might find yourself constantly second-guessing your gut feelings, struggling to trust the intuitive nudges that arise from within. This lack of faith in your inner compass can lead to a feeling of being lost or adrift, unsure of your life's direction. Overactive imaginations or difficulty focusing can also be signs of an imbalance. You might find yourself bombarded with a constant stream of thoughts and ideas, unable to sift through the noise and access the quieter voice of your intuition. This energetic congestion can lead to feelings of confusion, indecisiveness, and a disconnect from your inner wisdom, the very essence that guides you towards fulfillment.

The good news is that there are ways to clear and balance your third eye chakra, allowing you to tap into your intuition and see the world with greater clarity. Meditation is a powerful tool in this regard. Practices that focus on visualization can be particularly beneficial. Imagine yourself bathed in indigo light, the color associated with the third eye chakra. As you visualize this light filling your mind and expanding outwards, imagine it clearing away any energetic blockages and stimulating your intuition. Guided meditations that incorporate similar imagery can also be effective in awakening your third eye.

Spending time in nature can also be a potent way to nurture your third eye chakra. The vastness of nature has a way of putting things into perspective and sparking your inner wisdom. Look for natural environments that reflect the indigo color of the third eye chakra, such as bodies of water that mirror the clear blue sky. Surrounding yourself with the tranquility of nature allows your mind to settle, creating space for intuitive insights to emerge.

Engaging activities that challenge your mind and

encourage you to think creatively can also be a powerful tool for balancing your third eye chakra. Journaling prompts that ask you to explore your intuition or dream analysis exercises can help you connect with the symbolic language of your subconscious mind. Ultimately, by nurturing your third eye chakra, you cultivate a deeper sense of trust in your intuition and gain a clearer vision for your life's path. You become the master of your own destiny, guided by the unwavering light of your inner wisdom.

The **crown chakra**, Sahasrara in Sanskrit, sits at the very top of your head, symbolizing your connection to the divine or the universal energy. It represents enlightenment, spiritual awareness, and a sense of oneness with all things. When your crown chakra is balanced and its energy vibrates at a high frequency, you experience a deep sense of connection to something greater than yourself. You feel a sense of peace, unity, and boundless potential. This connection allows you to experience life with a sense of wonder and purpose.

Sahasrara is associated with the color violet and the element of spirit. Some believe it resonates with very high frequencies, nearing the range of light itself. Activities that promote a sense of awe and wonder, like gazing at the stars or contemplating the vastness of the universe, are thought to activate this chakra.

A blocked crown chakra can manifest in a sense of disconnection from something larger than yourself. You might feel lost, uninspired, or unable to find meaning in life. Cynicism or a closed mind can also be signs of an imbalance. This can lead to feelings of isolation, loneliness, and a lack of purpose. A blocked crown chakra can also manifest in headaches, dizziness, or feeling disconnected from your body.

Practices that focus on gratitude, compassion, or simply connecting with your breath can all be powerful tools for opening and activating your crown chakra. Gratitude meditation, for instance, involves focusing on the things you're thankful for in life. As you contemplate the blessings that surround you, a sense of positivity and contentment washes over you. This positive energy resonates with the high vibrational frequency of the crown chakra, gently nudging it towards a balanced state. Similarly, cultivating compassion, whether for yourself or others, fosters a sense of connection and oneness – qualities that lie at the very heart of the crown chakra. Even a simple practice like mindful breathing can be surprisingly effective. By focusing on your breath, you quiet the chatter of the mind and create space for a deeper connection with your spiritual essence.

Spending time in nature, particularly in serene and awe-inspiring settings, can also be a powerful tool for nurturing your crown chakra. The vastness of a mountain range, the tranquility of a silent forest, or the immensity of the ocean all have a way of humbling us and reminding us of our place in the grand scheme of the universe. Surrounding yourself with the beauty of nature allows you to quiet your mind and enter a state of openness. In this state of quietude, you become more receptive to the subtle energetic frequencies that permeate the universe, fostering a sense of connection with something larger than yourself.

Finally, practices that promote a sense of purpose and service to others can be very helpful in balancing your crown chakra. Volunteering your time at a local soup kitchen, helping a neighbor in need, or even simply performing random acts of kindness can all contribute to a feeling of connection to something larger than yourself. These acts of service nourish the spirit and allow you to experience the interconnectedness of all beings. Ultimately, by nurturing your crown chakra through practices like gratitude, spending time in nature, and acts of service, you cultivate a sense of peace, purpose, and a profound connection to the universe, allowing you to experience a sense of oneness with all things.

As you embark on the path of chakra clearing, you set yourself on a course of energetic alignment. Each chakra, functioning at its optimal level, vibrates with a specific frequency, contributing to a greater symphony of well-being. Imagine your chakras not as isolated instruments, but as an intricate orchestra. When each chakra plays its part in perfect harmony, the resulting music is a powerful and uplifting force. In the same way, a balanced chakra system allows your life force energy, known as prana, to flow freely and abundantly. This unobstructed flow nourishes your entire being, promoting physical vitality, emotional stability, and mental clarity.

This energetic coherence is not merely a passive state of internal balance. It is believed to raise your vibrational frequency, attuning you to a higher resonance with the universe. This doesn't necessarily mean achieving enlightenment overnight. Rather, it's a gradual process of becoming more receptive to the subtle energies that surround you. As your vibrational frequency rises, you foster a deeper connection to your inner wisdom, the inherent intelligence of your body, and the vast consciousness of the universe itself. This heightened awareness can blossom into a more fulfilling and meaningful life, where you experience a profound sense of connection to all that is. By tending to your chakras, you are not simply clearing blockages; you are cultivating a life that vibrates with authenticity, purpose, and a profound sense of belonging within the grand tapestry of existence.

Reiki

Reiki, an ancient Japanese healing technique, has emerged as a popular modality in the world of vibrational healing. It centers on the belief that an unseen life force energy flows through all living things. Proponents of Reiki believe that this energy, sometimes referred to as ki or universal life force, plays a vital role in our physical, emotional, and spiritual well-being. When this energy flows freely and smoothly, we experience a sense of balance and vitality. Conversely, blockages or imbalances in this energy flow are believed to contribute to disharmony and potential health issues.

Reiki's connection to vibrational healing and raising your vibration lies in its ability to influence the symphony of energetic frequencies that course through your body. Imagine these frequencies as the instruments in an orchestra. When your energy flows freely and unimpeded, each "instrument" vibrates at its optimal level, creating a harmonious and balanced composition. This symphony of balanced vibrations is believed to reflect a state of overall well-being.

However, blockages and imbalances in your energy flow can disrupt this harmonious resonance. Just as a detuned instrument throws off the entire orchestra's sound, energetic disruptions can create disharmonious vibrations within your body. These disharmonies may manifest not only as physical ailments but also as emotional distress and a general sense of dis-ease.

This is where Reiki's role becomes significant. By acting as a conduit for universal life force energy, a Reiki practitioner helps to clear these energetic blockages. Imagine Reiki like a gentle tuning fork, subtly resonating with your body's energy and encouraging it to return to its natural frequency. As blockages dissolve and the flow of energy becomes smoother, the symphony of vibrations within you begins to find its balance once more. This restored harmony is believed to raise your overall vibrational frequency, promoting a sense of well-being that extends beyond the physical realm. It's a return to a state of energetic coherence, where your body, mind, and spirit resonate together in a state of vibrant health and inner peace.

The connection between Reiki and vibrational healing extends beyond its ability to directly harmonize your energetic symphony. Reiki also plays a significant role in promoting relaxation and well-being, which can indirectly create an environment conducive to raising your vibrational frequency.

Imagine your body's energy as a flowing river. When you're stressed or tense, it's as if the riverbed becomes clogged with debris, restricting the flow of water. This stagnant energy can manifest as physical tension, emotional imbalances, and a general feeling of dis-ease. Reiki's calming effect acts like a gentle current, gradually clearing away these blockages and allowing your energy to flow more freely. As you surrender to the deep relaxation that Reiki often induces, your nervous system quiets, and the chatter of your mind begins to settle. This state of inner peace allows your body's natural healing mechanisms to come to the forefront, further promoting a return to energetic balance.

It's important to remember that the body possesses an inherent wisdom. When you're relaxed and centered, your body is better equipped to identify and address any underlying imbalances in your energy field. This creates a fertile ground for self-healing, allowing your vibrational frequency to rise organically. Reiki, by promoting relaxation and well-being, fosters an environment where this self-healing potential can truly flourish. It's a gentle nudge in the right direction, encouraging your body to return to its natural state of vibrant health and inner harmony – a state characterized by a higher vibrational frequency.

Reiki's influence extends far beyond its ability to harmonize your energy and promote relaxation. It fosters a holistic approach to well-being, impacting not only your energetic state but also your emotional and spiritual well-being. The deep relaxation and sense of peace that often washes over you during a Reiki session can have a profound ripple effect. As your body releases tension and your mind quiets, a space opens up for positive emotions to blossom. Feelings of self-compassion, gratitude, and connection can begin to take root.

These positive emotions are not simply fleeting

experiences. They carry a specific energetic signature, and when cultivated through practices like Reiki, they are believed to contribute to a higher vibrational state. Imagine your vibrational frequency as a lighthouse's beacon. When negative emotions like anger or fear dominate, the beacon's light becomes dim and distorted. However, as feelings of self-compassion, gratitude, and connection take hold, the beacon's light shines brighter and clearer, radiating a higher frequency.

This shift in your emotional landscape isn't simply a byproduct of relaxation. Reiki, by promoting a connection to your inner wisdom, can gently guide you towards self-awareness and higher consciousness. As you become more attuned to your thoughts and feelings, you gain the ability to identify and release negativity that might be weighing you down. This process of emotional release can be a powerful catalyst for personal growth, allowing you to cultivate a more positive outlook and a deeper sense of connection to yourself and the world around you. Ultimately, Reiki's holistic approach creates a fertile ground for a higher vibrational state, where your physical, emotional, and spiritual well-being resonate in harmonious alignment.

Stepping into a Reiki session is like entering a sanctuary designed to promote deep relaxation and holistic healing. The environment itself plays a crucial role in setting the stage for this transformative experience. Imagine a room bathed in soft, warm lighting, creating an inviting ambiance that immediately puts you at ease. Tranquil music might fill the air, gentle melodies that melt away stress and usher in a sense of serenity. The temperature is carefully regulated, neither too hot nor too cold, ensuring optimal comfort throughout the session. More than just physical comfort, this meticulously crafted environment fosters a sense of safety and security, a crucial element for allowing your body and mind to fully surrender to the healing potential of Reiki.

The practitioner themself becomes an embodiment of this calming presence. Their demeanor is warm and welcoming, radiating a sense of compassion and quiet strength. They'll likely invite you to either lie down on a comfortable massage table or sit in a chair, whichever position allows you to feel most at ease. There's no need to disrobe for a Reiki session; comfortable, loose-fitting clothing is perfectly acceptable. Before commencing the actual Reiki treatment, the practitioner will take some time to connect with you on a personal level. This initial conversation serves several purposes. It allows you to express your intentions for the session, whether you're seeking stress relief, addressing a specific physical issue, or simply promoting overall well-being. The practitioner will likely ask questions to gain a deeper understanding of your needs and tailor the session accordingly. This open communication helps establish trust and creates a safe space where you can feel comfortable expressing your vulnerabilities and expectations. By the time the Reiki treatment begins, you'll feel enveloped in a supportive and nurturing environment, fully prepared to embark on this journey of holistic healing.

As you settle comfortably on the massage table or in the chair, the Reiki practitioner begins the hands-on portion of the session. Their touch is light and gentle, a mere hovering over specific areas of your body or a soft placement with their palms resting flat. These precise positions correspond to your chakra points, those energetic centers believed to be swirling vortexes within your body. Imagine them as luminous gateways, pulsating with the life force energy that governs your physical, emotional, and spiritual well-being. The Reiki practitioner isn't dictating where this energy flows; instead, they act as a conduit, a clear channel for the Reiki energy to move intuitively. This universal energy is believed to possess a wisdom of its own, seeking out areas within your body that require healing or rebalancing.

Throughout the session, the practitioner might gently shift their hand placements, following the intuitive pull of the Reiki energy. Some areas might feel warm or tingly as the energy flows, while others may experience a sense of coolness or stillness. These are all normal occurrences, and there's no right or wrong way to feel during a Reiki session. The key is to simply allow yourself to be open and receptive to the healing energy that surrounds you.

It's important to remember that Reiki is not a massage; there's no pressure or manipulation of the muscles. The practitioner's touch is light and serves primarily as a way to connect with the energetic field of your body. As the Reiki flows, you might find your mind wandering or thoughts arising. Don't try to force these thoughts away;

simply acknowledge them and allow them to drift past like clouds in the sky. The goal is to enter a state of deep relaxation, where your body and mind can fully surrender to the restorative power of Reiki.

As the Reiki practitioner maintains these hand placements on your chakra points, a cascade of sensations might arise, although their presence or intensity varies from person to person. Some individuals describe a gentle warmth emanating from the practitioner's hands, a comforting sensation that seems to seep deep into their core. Imagine basking in a pool of sunshine, the warmth radiating outward, loosening any tension held within your muscles. Others might experience a tingling sensation, a subtle buzz that dances across the areas where the Reiki energy is most concentrated. This tingling can be invigorating, almost like a gentle awakening within your energetic body. In contrast, some people perceive a coolness, a refreshing wave that washes over them. This coolness isn't unpleasant; instead, it can signal a clearing or releasing of stagnant energy, making way for a renewed flow.

Beyond these physical sensations, you might also experience a shift in your internal energy landscape. Imagine a dam releasing pent-up pressure, creating a surge of energy that flows freely throughout your body. This shift can manifest as a feeling of lightness, a sense of being unburdened by emotional heaviness or physical discomfort. For others, a wave of deep relaxation washes over them, a profound sense of peace that permeates their being. This isn't simply drowsiness; it's a state of complete surrender, a letting go of worries and anxieties as you allow the Reiki to work its magic.

There's no right or wrong way to feel during a Reiki session. The beauty of this practice lies in its unique experience for each individual. Some people have vivid visualizations or emotional releases, while others simply drift off into a state of peaceful slumber. The key is to approach the session with an open mind and a receptive heart, allowing yourself to experience the Reiki energy in whatever way feels most natural for you.

As the Reiki treatment unfolds, many people describe it as a deeply relaxing journey. The practitioner's gentle hand placements and the calming environment all conspire to create a sanctuary for your mind and body. Imagine yourself enveloped in a warm cocoon of tranquility, where worries and anxieties melt away like snowflakes on a hot stove. In this state of serenity, you're encouraged to focus on your breath, a simple yet powerful anchor that draws your attention inwards. With each inhalation, feel a wave of peace wash over you, and with each exhalation, release any lingering tension or negativity. This isn't about forcing your mind into stillness; it's about allowing thoughts to arise and then gently letting them go, like leaves carried away by a gentle breeze. The more you surrender to this present moment, the deeper the relaxation becomes.

The effects of Reiki can extend far beyond the

confines of the treatment session. Many people report feeling a renewed sense of energy and well-being in the following hours or even days. Imagine waking up the next morning feeling lighter, more invigorated, and ready to tackle the day with newfound optimism. The deep relaxation you experienced during the session can linger, creating a sense of inner calm that allows you to navigate life's challenges with greater ease. Emotional shifts are also common after a Reiki session. You might feel more centered, grounded, and at peace with yourself and the world around you. This emotional equilibrium can empower you to approach situations with greater clarity and compassion.

It's important to note that not everyone experiences Reiki in the same way. While some people feel a surge of energy afterwards, others might experience a temporary dip in energy levels. This is sometimes referred to as a "healing crisis" and is believed to be a sign that your body is detoxifying and releasing stagnant energy. Similar to the physical discomfort you might experience after a workout as your muscles rebuild, this temporary fatigue is an indication of positive change within your energetic system. The key is to listen to your body and allow it the rest it needs to integrate the healing benefits of the Reiki treatment. Ultimately, whether you experience a surge of energy, a deep sense of peace, or even a temporary period of fatigue, these after-effects are all signs that the Reiki is prompting positive shifts within your being, moving you towards a state of greater balance and well-being.

Reiki's role in vibrational healing and consciousness lies in its ability to address the energetic foundation of well-being. By promoting a smooth flow of energy and reducing blockages, Reiki may contribute to a more harmonious symphony of vibrations within the body, potentially raising your overall vibrational frequency. Additionally, the deep relaxation and sense of peace fostered by Reiki can create an environment conducive to positive emotions and a more balanced state of being. Many find Reiki to be a valuable tool on their journey towards a more awakened state of consciousness. By promoting relaxation, reducing stress, and fostering a sense of inner peace, Reiki may pave the way for a more balanced and vibrant experience of life.

Meditation and Visualization

Meditation and visualization practices have become powerful tools for those seeking to explore the connection between mind, body, and vibrational energy. These techniques can be practiced independently or combined to create a personalized approach to vibrational healing and expanding consciousness.

In your journey towards a higher vibrational state, meditation and visualization can be powerful tools. Meditation, at its core, is the practice of cultivating present-moment awareness. Imagine your mind as a constantly chattering radio. Meditation helps you turn down the volume, allowing you to focus on the present moment, your breath, or a chosen mantra. This practice goes beyond mere relaxation; it's a path to self-discovery and a powerful tool for fostering a harmonious energetic state.

As you settle into meditation, focusing on your breath or mantra, thoughts and emotions inevitably arise. The key here isn't to suppress them but to observe them with a sense of detached awareness. Imagine these thoughts like clouds drifting across a vast blue sky. Acknowledge their presence but don't get caught up in their storm. By gently guiding your attention back to your breath or mantra, you gradually cultivate a sense of inner peace and quietude.

This inner stillness has a profound impact on your vibrational state. When your mind is calm and focused, the energy within your body is believed to become more harmonious and balanced. Think of it like an orchestra. With a scattered and agitated conductor (your mind), the instruments (your energy centers) can fall out of sync, creating disharmony. However, in a state of meditative calm, the conductor becomes centered, allowing each instrument to vibrate at its optimal frequency, resulting in a beautiful and cohesive sound. In the same way, a focused and peaceful mind allows your energy to flow more freely and resonate at a higher frequency, potentially contributing to a state of vibrant well-being.

Visualization techniques can further enhance this meditative state. Imagine a warm, white light emanating from within you, filling your body and clearing any energetic blockages. This visualization can deepen your relaxation and focus, promoting a sense of balance and inner peace that resonates at a higher vibrational level. By incorporating meditation and visualization into your practice, you cultivate a fertile ground for a higher vibrational state, where your physical, emotional, and spiritual well-being find harmonious alignment.

Building upon the foundation of inner calm established through meditation, visualization practices can become a powerful tool for influencing your vibrational state. Imagine your mind as a sculptor, and your thoughts and emotions as the clay. Through visualization, you actively shape this formless clay into specific experiences. By conjuring vivid mental imagery, you can directly influence your energy flow and emotional state.

For instance, visualize yourself bathed in white light, a color often associated with healing and purification. Let your mind paint a detailed picture of this light, soft and radiant, enveloping you completely. Feel the warmth of this light seep into your body, dissolving any tension or negativity it encounters. As you focus on this image, a wave of calmness washes over you. This visualization not only promotes relaxation but also encourages a shift in your energetic state towards a more harmonious and balanced frequency.

The power of visualization extends beyond relaxation. Imagine yourself surrounded by a vibrant meadow, filled with wildflowers and buzzing with life. Focus on the feeling of joy that this scene evokes within you. Perhaps visualize yourself reuniting with a loved one, or achieving a cherished goal. By anchoring yourself in these positive emotions, you harness their inherent energetic signature. Remember, emotions like joy, gratitude, and inner peace are believed to resonate at higher vibrational frequencies. Through visualization, you cultivate these emotions within yourself, potentially raising your overall vibrational state and promoting a sense of well-being that extends beyond the physical realm.

The benefits of meditation and visualization go beyond the immediate experience. By training your mind to focus and cultivating a sense of inner peace, these practices can have a lasting impact on your overall well-being. As you become more aware of your thoughts and emotions, you gain the ability to choose how you react to situations. This newfound sense of control and emotional balance can contribute to a more positive outlook and a higher vibrational state.

Furthermore, meditation and visualization can open doors to a deeper exploration of consciousness. By quieting the mind and focusing your awareness inward, you may experience a greater sense of connection to yourself and the world around you. This expansion of consciousness can be a powerful tool for personal growth and transformation, potentially leading to a more vibrant and fulfilling experience of life.

It's important to remember that these practices are not about achieving some perfect state of meditation or visualization. The key is to approach them with patience, curiosity, and a willingness to experiment. With consistent practice, you may discover how meditation and visualization can become powerful tools for raising your vibration, fostering inner peace, and expanding your consciousness.

Aromatherapy

Aromatherapy, the practice of using essential oils for therapeutic purposes, offers a fascinating approach to vibrational healing. These potent plant extracts are believed to not only influence our sense of smell but also interact with our bodies on a subtler energetic level. Here's how aromatherapy might play a role in raising your vibration and consciousness.

The essence of aromatherapy lies in the complex chemical makeup of essential oils. These oils contain a multitude of aromatic compounds, each vibrating at a specific frequency. When we inhale these oils, the aromatic molecules interact with olfactory receptors in the nose, sending signals to the brain. This not only influences our sense of smell but may also trigger emotional and physiological responses.

Proponents of vibrational healing believe that essential oils can also interact with our energy field. Imagine each essential oil vibrating at its unique frequency. When inhaled or applied topically, these frequencies are believed to resonate with the body's energy centers, potentially influencing the flow of energy and promoting a more harmonious state. For example, the uplifting aroma of citrus oils like lemon or orange might introduce a higher frequency, promoting feelings of joy and alertness, which may in turn raise your overall vibrational state.

When we inhale these aromatic molecules, they may influence our own energetic landscape. The calming scent of lavender oil, for example, is believed to resonate at a frequency that promotes relaxation and inner peace. Inhaling lavender may help to gently nudge our own energy towards a more harmonious and balanced state, potentially raising our overall vibrational frequency.

This interaction goes beyond the physical sense of smell. When applied topically, essential oils are absorbed to a limited degree through the skin. Proponents believe this absorption allows the plant's vibrational signature to interact with our energy field on a more direct level. However, it's important to remember to dilute essential oils properly before topical application to avoid skin irritation.

The key to incorporating aromatherapy into your vibrational healing journey lies in experimentation and intuition. Research the specific properties of different essential oils and choose ones that resonate with your intentions. Perhaps you seek a sense of grounding and focus; in that case, essential oils like sandalwood or cedarwood might be appropriate. If feelings of joy and creativity are your goal, citrus oils like lemon or grapefruit could be beneficial. Trust your intuition when selecting and using essential oils, allowing them to guide you towards a more balanced and vibrant energetic state.

However, the relationship between essential oils

and vibrational healing isn't a one-size-fits-all approach. Certain oils, like invigorating citrus scents, are believed to vibrate at higher frequencies. Inhaling these uplifting aromas, like lemon or grapefruit, may introduce a higher vibrational frequency into our energy field, promoting alertness and focus. This suggests a fascinating possibility: by strategically selecting essential oils based on their vibrational properties, we can potentially influence our own energetic state, shifting it up or down the vibrational scale to achieve a desired outcome.

The key to incorporating aromatherapy effectively lies in experimentation and intuition. Research the specific properties of different essential oils and choose ones that resonate with your intentions. Perhaps you seek a sense of grounding and focus; sandalwood or cedarwood might be appropriate choices. If feelings of joy and creativity are your goal, citrus oils could be beneficial.

Delving deeper into the fascinating world of vibrational healing and aromatherapy, we discover a profound connection between scent and our emotional landscape. Our sense of smell holds a unique position within our sensory system. Unlike other senses, like sight or sound, olfactory information travels directly to the limbic system, the primitive part of the brain that governs our emotions and memory. This direct pathway allows essential oils, with their potent aromatic profiles, to trigger powerful emotional responses.

Imagine inhaling the uplifting scent of citrus, a

fruit explosion of sunshine and joy. As the essential oil molecules reach your olfactory receptors, they send a message straight to your limbic system. This part of your brain recognizes the citrus aroma, potentially triggering a cascade of positive emotions – feelings of joy, optimism, and perhaps even a surge of creativity. These emotions we experience are not simply fleeting psychological states; they are believed to carry a specific energetic signature, a unique vibrational frequency. When emotions like joy and optimism take center stage, they influence the overall vibration of your energetic field. Inhaling citrus oil, or any essential oil that evokes positive emotions, could potentially nudge your vibrational frequency upwards, promoting a sense of well-being that resonates throughout your being.

The influence of essential oils extends beyond triggering positive emotions. Certain scents can evoke powerful memories. Perhaps the aroma of lavender reminds you of a calming bedtime ritual from your childhood, or the earthy scent of sandalwood brings back memories of a peaceful meditation session. These emotional connections we have with certain scents can be harnessed to shift our energetic state. By inhaling an essential oil linked to a positive memory, you might experience a sense of relaxation, peace, or a renewed sense of grounding – emotional states that are believed to resonate at lower vibrational frequencies. In this way, aromatherapy offers a unique tool for emotional self-regulation, allowing you to use scent to consciously influence your energetic state and promote a sense of vibrational harmony.

Aromatherapy can also be used in conjunction with other practices that promote a higher vibration. For example, diffusing a calming essential oil like lavender during meditation can create a more relaxing environment, potentially deepening your experience and promoting a more balanced energetic state.

Many people find aromatherapy to be a powerful and beneficial practice. The combination of fragrance, topical application, and the emotional connection we have with scents can create a unique experience that promotes relaxation, emotional well-being, and a sense of inner peace. By creating this balanced and positive state, aromatherapy may contribute to raising your overall vibrational frequency.

Here's a breakdown of some common aromatherapy fragrances and their influence on vibrational healing and energy frequencies:

Calming and Balancing:

- **Lavender:** As mentioned previously, lavender promotes relaxation and stress reduction, lowering your vibrational frequency to a balanced state.
- **Chamomile:** Similar to lavender, chamomile offers calming properties and tranquility corresponding with a lower, balanced vibrational frequency.
- **Sandalwood:** This grounding oil promotes inner peace and emotional stability, contributing to a more balanced

vibrational state.

- **Cedarwood:** Known for its calming and grounding aroma, cedarwood can ease anxiety and promote feelings of security, lowering your vibrational frequency to a relaxed state.
- **Ylang Ylang:** This floral oil offers stress-relieving properties and can promote feelings of peace and emotional balance, influencing a balanced vibrational state.
- **Bergamot:** Uplifting yet calming, bergamot oil can ease anxiety and promote relaxation, creating a sense of emotional balance that correspond with a balanced vibrational frequency.

Uplifting and Energizing:

- **Citrus Oils (Lemon, Orange, Grapefruit):** These invigorating scents promote alertness, focus, and optimism, introducing a higher vibrational frequency.
- **Rosemary:** Enhancing focus and mental clarity, rosemary's sharp scent corresponds with a higher vibrational frequency, promoting alertness and cognitive function.
- **Peppermint:** Combating fatigue and improving mental alertness, peppermint oil's stimulating aroma is believed to introduce a higher vibrational frequency.
- **Lemongrass:** Known for its uplifting and energizing properties, lemongrass oil can combat lethargy and promote a sense of renewed energy, influencing a higher vibrational frequency.
- **Spearmint:** Similar to peppermint,

spearmint offers an invigorating aroma that can promote alertness and focus, influencing a higher vibrational frequency.

- **Eucalyptus:** This stimulating oil can clear the mind and enhance mental clarity, influencing a higher vibrational frequency associated with alertness.

Grounding and Centering:

- **Sandalwood:** As mentioned earlier, sandalwood promotes inner peace and emotional stability, contributing to a balanced and grounded state.
- **Patchouli:** This earthy oil offers grounding and centering properties, promoting a sense of stability and emotional balance, influencing a balanced vibrational state.
- **Vetiver:** Known for its grounding and calming effects, vetiver oil can ease anxiety and promote emotional stability, contributing to a balanced vibrational state.
- **Frankincense:** This uplifting and grounding oil promotes feelings of peace, clarity, and focus. It influences a balanced vibrational state due to its calming yet stimulating properties.
- **Cedarwood:** In addition to its calming properties, cedarwood oil can also promote feelings of security and emotional grounding, contributing to a balanced vibrational state.

The way essential oils affect you can be individual. Experiment and find the fragrances that resonate most with you. Always use high-quality, therapeutic-grade oils diluted with a carrier oil for safe topical application. By incorporating aromatherapy into your self-care routine, you can explore the potential to raise your vibrational frequency and cultivate a more balanced and vibrant life.

Crystal Therapy

Crystal therapy invites us to explore the world of minerals and their potential to influence our well-being through vibration. Crystals possess unique energetic signatures, specific frequencies that resonate within their very structure. By interacting with these crystals, perhaps by holding them, placing them on the body, or simply being in their presence, we may be able to influence our own energy flow and vibrational state.

In the realm of vibrational healing, crystals take center stage as tools believed to interact with our energetic field. Imagine each crystal as a tiny tuning fork, vibrating at a specific frequency, a unique signature that reflects its inherent energetic properties. When we hold a crystal or place it on our body, we enter into a subtle energetic exchange. This interaction influences our own energy field, promoting a more harmonious flow and raising our overall vibrational frequency.

Think of your body's energy as a complex symphony, with each chakra acting as an instrument. When energy flows freely and unimpeded, the resulting symphony resonates with a sense of well-being. However, blockages or imbalances within your energy field can disrupt this harmonious flow, creating dissonant notes within the symphony. Crystals, with their specific vibrational frequencies, are believed to act as tuning forks for your energy field.

For instance, a rose quartz crystal is known for its gentle and loving energy. It vibrates at a frequency that resonates with feelings of love, compassion, and emotional healing. Holding a rose quartz crystal or placing it on your chest during meditation could potentially introduce this harmonious frequency into your energy field. This, in turn, might help to dissolve blockages associated with negative emotions like anger or resentment, ultimately promoting a smoother flow of energy and potentially raising your vibrational frequency to a state of greater love and acceptance.

Crystal therapy offers a unique perspective on how these beautiful minerals can interact with our energetic field. The core principle lies in the belief that each crystal vibrates at a specific frequency, an energetic signature that reflects its inherent properties. When imbalances or blockages arise within our energy field, they can manifest not only as emotional distress but also as physical ailments. Crystals, with their unique vibrational frequencies, are believed to act as tools to clear these blockages and promote a more balanced flow of energy.

Imagine your energy field as a flowing river. Ideally, the water courses smoothly and freely, nourishing the landscape it touches. However, blockages or imbalances can act like dams, restricting the flow and creating stagnant pockets of energy. These stagnant areas are believed to contribute to disharmony within the body, potentially manifesting as emotional turmoil or physical discomfort. Smoky quartz, for instance, is renowned for its grounding and detoxifying properties. It vibrates at a frequency that resonates with cleansing and renewal. By holding a smoky quartz crystal or placing it on the body during meditation, you might introduce this cleansing energy into your stagnant energy field. This, in turn, could help to dissolve blockages and promote a smoother flow of energy throughout your system. As the energetic dam is cleared, the river begins to flow freely once more, potentially alleviating the physical or emotional discomfort associated with the blockage and contributing to a more balanced and vibrant energetic state.

Crystal therapy goes beyond the simple notion of crystals possessing specific energetic properties. An important aspect of this practice lies in the power of intention and focus. Imagine a crystal as a beautiful conduit, waiting to be activated by your conscious will. By setting a clear intention for what you wish to achieve, such as increased clarity or emotional balance, you imbue the crystal with your focused energy.

The act of setting an intention is a powerful act of self-awareness. As you hold the crystal and contemplate your desired outcome, you bring your attention to the specific area you wish to address. This focused awareness itself can be a catalyst for positive change. By directing your mental energy towards clarity, for instance, you might begin to identify and release thought patterns that have been clouding your mind. Similarly, focusing on emotional balance with the aid of a crystal could encourage the release of negativity and foster a sense of inner peace.

This mindful approach goes beyond simply amplifying the crystal's influence. The act of setting an intention and focusing your attention on the crystal creates a powerful synergy. Your focused energy interacts with the crystal's unique vibration, potentially creating a ripple effect within your own energetic field. Remember, emotions themselves are believed to carry a specific vibrational frequency. By consciously cultivating positive emotions like clarity or inner peace through your focused intention and interaction with the crystal, you may be influencing your overall vibrational state. The crystal acts as a tool, helping you elevate your emotional landscape to a higher frequency, a state that resonates more with well-being and aligns with your desired outcome.

It's important to remember that crystals are not meant to be a quick fix. Their influence is subtle and unfolds over time. By carrying a specific crystal throughout the day, meditating with crystals placed on your chakras, or simply spending time in their presence, you allow their unique vibrations to gently interact with your energy field. This consistent interaction is believed to create a cumulative effect, fostering a more balanced and vibrant energetic state, ultimately contributing to a sense of well-being that extends beyond the physical realm.

Here's a look at some crystals and their connection to vibrational healing and energy frequencies:

Grounding and Balancing:

- **Smoky Quartz:** As mentioned previously, smoky quartz promotes grounding and detoxification, clearing blockages and contributing to a balanced vibrational state.
- **Black Tourmaline:** This protective stone shields against negativity and fosters emotional stability, influencing a balanced vibrational state.
- **Amethyst:** This calming crystal promotes peace, reduces anxiety, and enhances intuition. A calmer emotional state resonates at a more balanced vibrational frequency.
- **Hematite:** Known for its grounding properties, hematite promotes security, focus, and self-confidence. This emotional stability contributes to a balanced vibrational state.
- **Obsidian:** This volcanic glass offers grounding and protection. It's believed to help clear negativity and promote emotional balance, influencing a balanced vibrational state.

Stimulating and Uplifting:

- **Citrine:** The "success stone" promotes abundance, creativity, and motivation. Its optimistic energy influences a higher vibrational frequency.
- **Carnelian:** This energizing crystal stimulates motivation, creativity, and courage. This increase in vitality and positive emotions correspond with a

higher vibrational frequency.

- **Tiger's Eye:** Enhancing mental clarity, focus, and willpower, tiger's eye influences a higher vibrational state associated with alertness and mental focus.
- **Yellow Jasper:** Associated with joy and optimism, yellow jasper's bright energy influences a higher vibrational frequency.
- **Orange Calcite:** This energizing crystal promotes creativity, joy, and motivation. These positive emotions contribute to a higher vibrational state.

Cleansing and Purification:

- **Clear Quartz:** Often called the "master healer," clear quartz is believed to amplify energy and intention. It might cleanse and purify your energy field, promoting a balanced vibrational state.
- **Selenite:** This white crystal is known for its cleansing properties. It's believed to clear negativity and promote mental clarity, influencing a balanced vibrational state.

Heart Chakra and Love:

- **Rose Quartz:** The "love stone" promotes emotional healing, self-love, and compassion. A state of love and acceptance resonates at a higher vibrational frequency.
- **Green Aventurine:** Associated with love, abundance, and growth, green aventurine's positive energy might

influence a higher vibrational frequency.
- **Malachite:** This vibrant green stone promotes emotional balance, transformation, and releasing negativity. A state of emotional well-being contributes to a higher vibrational state.

The way crystals affect you can be individual. Experiment and find the crystals that resonate with you most. By incorporating crystals into your self-care routine and focusing on your intentions while holding them, you can explore their potential to promote relaxation, emotional well-being, and a sense of inner peace. These positive states may contribute to raising your overall vibrational frequency and cultivating a more vibrant life.

When it comes to using crystals for vibrational healing and potentially raising your energy frequency or consciousness, there's a beautiful interplay between intuition and intention.

Choosing crystals can be a deeply personal experience. While there are many resources suggesting specific crystals for different goals, the most important factor might be your own inner compass. Hold various crystals, pay attention to how they feel in your hand, and notice any emotional or energetic shifts you experience. This intuitive connection can guide you towards crystals that resonate most with you.

Once you've selected a few crystals that call to you, research their traditional uses and properties. Understanding their potential benefits can help you focus your intentions when working with them. Crystals are believed to absorb and emit energy, so it's generally recommended to cleanse them regularly to remove any stagnant energy they may have picked up. Smudging with sage, placing them in moonlight, or soaking them in saltwater (depending on the crystal) are some common cleansing methods. You can also charge your crystals by placing them in sunlight or moonlight, depending on their properties.

There are many ways to incorporate crystals into your self-care routine. During meditation, hold your chosen crystal and focus on your breath and intention, allowing the crystal's energy to support your practice. Crystal grids, where crystals are arranged in specific geometric patterns, can create a focused field of energy.

For targeted work, crystals can be placed on specific points on your body, such as your chakras (energy centers). You can also keep a tumbled stone or small crystal in your pocket or purse throughout the day as a reminder of your intention and to receive the crystal's subtle influence. Wearing crystal jewelry is another beautiful way to keep the crystal's energy close to you.

The key to using crystals effectively lies in approaching them with a sense of relaxation and focus. The more present and mindful you are, the more likely you are to experience their subtle influence. Remember, the power of crystals is partly rooted in the belief system surrounding them.

Using crystals for vibrational healing is an individualized practice. Experiment, find what resonates with you, and enjoy the journey of discovering their potential to elevate your sense of well-being.

Magnet Therapy

Magnet therapy dives into the world of magnetism and its potential to influence our well-being. It involves applying static magnetic fields from permanent magnets directly to the body. The belief is that our bodies are influenced by magnetic fields, both from Earth and from within our own cells. When these magnetic fields become imbalanced or disrupted, it's thought to manifest as physical or emotional issues.

Magnet therapy suggests that applying magnets to specific areas can restore balance within these magnetic fields. This, in turn, could promote a smoother flow of energy within the body influencing our overall vibrational state and raising our energy frequency.

The core principle of Magnet Therapy lies in the idea that every cell within our body vibrates at a specific frequency, a reflection of its health and function. Proponents of magnet therapy believe that applying magnets to specific areas of the body introduces an external magnetic field. This external field interacts with the vibrational state of our cells, promoting a more harmonious state.

Imagine your body as an intricate network of trillions of tiny living cells. Each cell vibrates with its own unique energy, and when all these vibrations are in sync, you experience a state of overall well-being. However, imbalances or disruptions within these cells can cause their vibrations to become erratic, similar to a discordant note. Magnet therapy suggests that magnets can influence these cellular vibrations. The specific magnetic field generated by the magnets is believed to gently nudge the cellular energy towards a more balanced and harmonious state, promoting overall health.

Think about placing a magnet on an area of tension or discomfort. The magnetic field might influence the vibrational state of the surrounding cells, promoting a more balanced flow of energy within that area. This, in turn, could potentially alleviate discomfort or tension by restoring a sense of cellular harmony. Additionally, a more harmonious cellular state can contribute to a higher overall vibrational frequency for the body. Just as a well-rehearsed orchestra resonates with a powerful and pleasing sound, a body composed of healthy, vibrantly functioning cells is believed to resonate at a higher frequency, potentially promoting a sense of overall well-being and vitality.

This influence extends beyond the physical. Our emotional state is also believed to resonate at a specific vibrational frequency. When we experience pain or discomfort, it can trigger a cascade of negative emotions like frustration or anxiety. These negative emotions can be seen as a lowering of our overall vibrational state.

Magnet therapy, by potentially reducing pain and promoting tissue healing, may create a foundation for a more positive emotional landscape. As the physical discomfort lessens, a natural shift can occur. Imagine the relief you feel when a pain point eases – a headache fades or a sore muscle recovers. This physical ease creates space for a more positive emotional state to emerge. Gratitude for the newfound comfort or a sense of calm contentment might arise. These positive emotions, like joy, gratitude, or simply a feeling of peace, are believed to resonate at a higher vibrational frequency.

By promoting a balanced cellular state and reducing pain, it can create a foundation for higher vibrational emotions to flourish. This shift fosters a sense of well-being that resonates on multiple levels, creating a more balanced and harmonious state of being.

When you experience pain or discomfort, it acts like a crack, allowing your vital energy to slowly leak out. This depletion can leave you feeling drained, both physically and emotionally. Magnet therapy, by potentially reducing pain and promoting relaxation, functions like a patch for that crack. As the physical discomfort lessens and your muscles begin to relax, the flow of energy within your body is no longer impeded. This newfound sense of ease allows your wellspring to replenish, restoring your energy reserves.

With your energy reserves restored, a shift in your emotional and mental state can occur. Think about the last time you finally unwound after a long and stressful day. As your body relaxes, your mind often quiets as well. This sense of calm creates fertile ground for cultivating positive intentions and a sense of inner peace. These positive emotions aren't simply fleeting psychological states; they are believed to resonate at higher vibrational frequencies.

Magnet therapy sessions involve applying the static magnetic fields of permanent magnets directly to your body. The idea is that our bodies respond to magnetic fields, both from the Earth and from within our own cells. When these internal fields become imbalanced, it's believed to manifest as physical or emotional issues. Magnet therapy aims to restore balance by placing magnets on specific areas.

There are two main ways magnet therapy is applied. Magnets can be placed directly on the area of concern, like a sore muscle or a joint. Alternatively, they can be positioned on specific acupressure points, believed to influence energy flow within the body. The strength of the magnets is measured in units called Gauss (Gs) or Tesla (T), and the recommended duration of use can vary depending on the issue and the type of magnet. Some people might wear a magnet for a few hours daily, while others use them continuously.

It's important to remember that magnet therapy is generally considered safe for most people, but there are some precautions. Pregnant women, people with pacemakers or other implanted medical devices, and anyone with severe bleeding disorders should avoid it. Consulting with a healthcare professional before starting magnet therapy is always a wise step, especially if you have any underlying health conditions.

Some practitioners utilize devices that generate pulsed electromagnetic fields (PEMFs) instead of static magnets. PEMFs are believed to have a more stimulating effect on tissues. However, magnet therapy itself uses static magnetic fields from permanent magnets.

Here's a closer look at some common areas targeted by magnet therapy and how they might relate to raising your energy frequency:

- **Lower Back:** Lower back pain can be a major drain on our energy. Magnet therapy applied here is believed to promote relaxation of muscles and improve circulation. This improved circulation and reduced tension could create a more balanced and comfortable state within the body, potentially contributing to a higher vibrational frequency.
- **Knees and Joints:** Sore knees and joints can restrict movement and create feelings of sluggishness. Magnets on these areas are thought to ease discomfort by promoting relaxation and reducing inflammation. Increased mobility and a reduction in pain could lead to a more positive emotional state and lighter physical feeling, both of which are believed to resonate at higher vibrational frequencies.
- **Headaches and Migraines:** The throbbing pain of headaches and migraines can be incredibly draining. Magnet therapy on the forehead or temples is believed to promote relaxation

and improve blood flow, potentially reducing pain intensity and frequency. A reduction in pain and tension could create a more balanced and comfortable state within the body, potentially contributing to a higher vibrational frequency.

- **Acupressure Points:** Acupressure points are believed to be key junctions along the body's energy pathways. Magnet therapy, when combined with acupressure, can target specific points to address various issues. By placing magnets on acupressure points associated with energy flow, relaxation, or specific organs, some people experience relief from issues like anxiety, insomnia, and nausea. Addressing these imbalances and promoting a smoother flow of energy could contribute to a more balanced and energized state, potentially raising your overall vibrational frequency.

Wearing magnet jewelry has also become a popular way to integrate magnet therapy into daily life for potential energy healing. The idea is that the magnets interact with your body's natural magnetic fields, potentially influencing energy flow and raising your overall vibrational state. Magnet jewelry offers a convenient and discreet approach. Bracelets, necklaces, and even earrings can be designed with hidden magnets, allowing for continuous or targeted magnetic field exposure throughout the day.

Similar to other forms of magnet therapy, intention plays a role here. Choosing a magnet jewelry piece that resonates with you and focusing on your desired outcome (pain relief, relaxation, etc.) while wearing it may amplify the potential benefits.

There are some additional things to consider. Comfort and quality are important factors. Choose magnet jewelry made with high-quality materials that feels comfortable to wear. The strength of the magnets can vary, so consider your preferences and consult a healthcare professional if you have any concerns.

In essence, magnet therapy may not only address the physical discomfort but also indirectly contribute to a more positive emotional and mental state. By potentially alleviating pain, promoting relaxation, and restoring your energy reserves, it creates an environment conducive to cultivating higher vibrational emotions. This shift fosters a sense of well-being that resonates on multiple levels, promoting a more balanced and harmonious state of being.

Ayurveda

Stepping into the rich tapestry of ancient healing traditions, Ayurveda stands out as a pillar of holistic well-being. Originating in India over 3,000 years ago, this traditional system of medicine offers a unique perspective on health and harmony. At its core lies the fundamental principle of interconnection – the idea that mind, body, and spirit are not separate entities but rather interwoven threads in the fabric of human existence. According to Ayurveda, true health arises when these interconnected aspects are balanced and function in concert.

This emphasis on balance extends to every facet of Ayurvedic practice. From dietary recommendations to lifestyle choices and herbal remedies, the aim is to identify and address any imbalances that may be contributing to disharmony within the individual. Just as a well-tuned orchestra relies on each instrument playing its part in perfect harmony, Ayurveda seeks to ensure that all aspects of the self – physical, mental, and spiritual – resonate together to create a symphony of well-being.

This holistic approach also places a strong emphasis on prevention. Ayurveda believes that disharmony, if left unchecked, can eventually manifest as disease. Therefore, a core principle involves identifying potential imbalances early on and taking proactive steps to maintain a state of balance. By following Ayurvedic practices, you can cultivate a lifestyle that nourishes not only your physical body but also your mind and spirit, fostering a sense of well-being that extends far beyond the absence of disease.

Unveiling the intricate workings of Ayurveda, the concept of Doshas takes center stage. These three unique energies, Vata, Pitta, and Kapha, are believed to be the fundamental building blocks of our physical and mental makeup. Imagine them as the primary colors on an artist's palette, each with its own distinct properties. Vata, composed of air and space, embodies movement, creativity, and lightness. Pitta, a fiery blend of fire and water, is associated with energy, transformation, and passion. Kapha, the grounded energy of earth and water, represents stability, structure, and nourishment.

According to Ayurveda, these Doshic energies exist within everyone in varying proportions, creating a unique blueprint for our individual constitution. This blueprint influences not only our physical characteristics but also our personality traits, tendencies, and even our susceptibility to certain imbalances. Just as a painting loses its vibrancy when the primary colors are out of balance, so too can our well-being suffer when our Doshas fall out of harmony. An excess of Vata might manifest as restlessness and anxiety, while an imbalance of Pitta could lead to irritability and digestive issues. Kapha imbalances, on the other hand, can present as sluggishness and emotional congestion.

Ayurveda emphasizes the importance of maintaining a balance between these Doshas for optimal health and well-being. This balance is not about achieving a static state but rather fostering a dynamic harmony. Imagine a skilled artist who mixes and blends the primary colors to create a masterpiece. In the same way, Ayurvedic practices aim to provide you with the tools to identify your unique Doshic constitution and any potential imbalances. Through dietary modifications, herbal remedies, lifestyle adjustments, and practices like yoga and meditation, you can learn to nurture your dominant Dosha while gently bringing the others into balance. This process of restoring Doshic harmony is believed to be not just about addressing physical ailments but also about raising your overall energy frequency and consciousness.

While there isn't a definitive way to diagnose your dominant dosha without professional guidance, Ayurveda offers some self-assessment methods to get a general idea. These methods are based on physical and psychological characteristics. Here's a breakdown to help you identify your potential dosha:

Vata Dosha:

- **Physical characteristics:** Slender or thin frame, dry skin, hair that's prone to dryness or frizz, digestion can be irregular, cold hands and feet.
- **Psychological characteristics:** Energetic but can get easily depleted,

creative and quick-thinking, spacey or
forgetful at times, difficulty sleeping.

Pitta Dosha:

- **Physical characteristics:** Medium build,
  sharp features, warm skin tone, oily hair,
  prone to heartburn or acidity, gets hot
  easily.
- **Psychological characteristics:** Sharp
  intellect, ambitious and driven,
  competitive, can be short-tempered or
  impatient, good leadership skills.

Kapha Dosha:

- **Physical characteristics:** Strong and
  sturdy build, thick or oily skin, hair tends
  to be thick and lustrous, good digestion,
  sleeps soundly.
- **Psychological characteristics:** Calm
  and grounded, patient and reliable,
  dislikes change, can be slow to make
  decisions, tends to hold onto things.

Important to Consider:

- Most people have a combination of all
  three doshas, but one or two are usually
  dominant.
- These characteristics are a general guide,
  and individual variations exist.
- Your dosha can change throughout your
  life based on factors like age, diet, and
  lifestyle.

Additional Tips:

- Observe your energy levels throughout the day. Are you most energetic in the morning (Vata), mid-day (Pitta), or evening (Kapha)?
- Consider your cravings and aversions towards certain foods. Vata might crave warm, grounding foods, Pitta might prefer cooling foods, and Kapha might crave light and stimulating foods (opposites of their dosha).
- Notice your emotional responses. Vata might experience anxiety or difficulty focusing, Pitta might be prone to anger or frustration, and Kapha might be slow to react or resistant to change.

By aligning your lifestyle with your Doshic nature, you cultivate a sense of inner peace and vitality. This newfound harmony is believed to resonate at a higher vibrational frequency, promoting a sense of well-being that extends beyond the physical realm. Additionally, Ayurvedic practices like meditation and yoga are well known for their ability to cultivate mindfulness and focus. As you quiet the mind and connect with your inner self, you raise your level of consciousness, fostering a deeper understanding of yourself and the world around you. In essence, Ayurveda offers a roadmap to a life that is not only free from disease but also vibrant, expansive, and connected, resonating at a higher frequency on multiple levels.

Unveiling the practical applications of Ayurveda, diet takes center stage as a powerful tool for promoting balance and well-being. According to Ayurvedic principles, the food we consume is not simply sustenance; it acts as a form of information, influencing our internal environment on a subtle yet profound level. Each food is believed to possess specific energetic qualities that can either aggravate or pacify certain Doshas. Imagine spices like ginger and black pepper – their fiery nature is seen as aggravating Pitta, the Dosha associated with heat and metabolism. Conversely, cooling and grounding vegetables like cucumber and leafy greens are considered pacifying for Pitta.

An Ayurvedic practitioner, trained in the art of Doshic identification, can assess your unique constitution and recommend a personalized diet tailored to your specific needs. This personalized approach goes beyond simply counting calories or following a fad diet. The focus is on aligning your dietary choices with your Doshic makeup to promote harmony within your body and mind. By consuming foods that pacify your dominant Dosha and minimize those that aggravate it, you create an internal environment conducive to optimal health.

This dietary approach, when combined with other Ayurvedic practices, is believed to contribute to raising your overall energy frequency and consciousness. Think of your body as a complex instrument. When you fuel it with the right foods – foods that resonate with your Doshic nature – you are essentially tuning the instrument for optimal performance. This balanced internal environment fosters a smoother flow of energy throughout your system, promoting a sense of vitality and well-being. The increased energy you experience is not simply physical; it's believed to translate into a higher vibrational state.

Here's a breakdown of some common Ayurvedic foods for each dosha that can help raise your energy frequency:

Vata Dosha: People with dominant Vata are often described as energetic, creative, and quick learners. However, imbalanced Vata can manifest as fatigue, anxiety, and difficulty sleeping.

- **Favorable foods:** Warm, cooked, and grounding foods are recommended. Think sweet, sour, and salty tastes. Examples include:
    - Sweet fruits: Dates, figs, raisins (in moderation)
    - Sweet vegetables: Sweet potatoes, winter squash, beets
    - Grains: Basmati rice, quinoa, oats
    - Nuts and seeds: Almonds, pumpkin seeds, sunflower seeds
    - Spices: Ginger, cinnamon, cumin, fennel

Pitta Dosha: Pitta individuals are known for their sharp intellect, leadership qualities, and ambitious nature. When imbalanced, Pitta can lead to irritability, digestive issues, and excessive heat in the body.

- **Favorable foods:** Cooling and soothing foods are key. Opt for bitter, sweet, and astringent tastes. Examples include:
    - Fruits: Watermelon, melons, pears,

apples (sweet varieties)
    - Vegetables: Leafy greens, cucumber, asparagus, broccoli
    - Grains: Basmati rice, barley, millet
    - Dairy: Ghee (clarified butter) in moderation
    - Spices: Coriander, fennel, cardamom, turmeric

Kapha Dosha: Kapha people tend to be calm, grounded, and naturally strong. Imbalances in Kapha can lead to sluggishness, weight gain, and congestion.

- **Favorable foods:** Light, warming, and stimulating foods are beneficial. Choose pungent, bitter, and astringent tastes. Examples include:
    - Fruits: Apples (tart varieties), cranberries, pomegranates
    - Vegetables: Cruciferous vegetables (cauliflower, broccoli, Brussels sprouts), leafy greens, celery
    - Grains: Millet, quinoa, amaranth
    - Spices: Ginger, black pepper, cayenne pepper (in moderation), cumin
    - Legumes: Mung beans, lentils (in moderation)

Ayurveda extends far beyond dietary practices, blossoming into a holistic approach to life itself. It acknowledges the interconnectedness of mind, body, and spirit, and aims to cultivate harmony within this delicate triad. Practices like yoga and meditation are central tenets of Ayurveda, not merely complementary exercises.

Yoga, with its emphasis on mindful movement and breathwork, serves as a powerful tool for calming the ever-churning mind. As you flow through a series of postures, your attention is drawn inwards, quieting the chatter of thoughts and anxieties. This quieting of the mind isn't simply about achieving relaxation; it's about creating space for a deeper connection with your inner self. Imagine peeling back the layers of external stimuli to reveal the quiet wisdom that resides within.In Ayurveda, yoga postures can be chosen to specifically balance each Dosha.

For Vata, the air and space Dosha, yoga emphasizes grounding and stability. Poses that focus on strengthening the core and legs, like Mountain Pose (Tadasana) or Warrior Poses (Virabhadrasana), can be beneficial. Forward bends and twists, however, should be approached with caution for Vata individuals, as they can increase airiness and space in the body. Child's Pose (Balasana) or Squat (Malasana) are examples of gentler postures that can promote feelings of security and stability.

Pitta, the fire and water Dosha, is balanced with yoga that cools and calms the fiery energy. Cooling postures like Moon Salutations (Chandra Namaskara) or Downward-Facing Dog (Adho Mukha Svanasana) can be helpful. Twisting poses, such as Half Lord of the Fishes Pose (Ardha Matsyendrasana), and gentle backbends, like Cat-Cow Pose (Marjaryasana-Bitilasana), can also be incorporated. These poses can reduce Pitta's fiery energy and promote feelings of peace and relaxation.

For Kapha, the earth and water Dosha, yoga aims to energize and stimulate the body and mind. Sun Salutations (Surya Namaskara) are a great option, along with standing poses like Warrior Poses (Virabhadrasana) or Triangle Pose (Trikonasana). Core strengthening exercises like Boat Pose (Navasana) can also be beneficial. These poses can help to ignite Kapha's energy and promote feelings of lightness and vitality.

Meditation, another cornerstone of Ayurvedic practice, takes this inner exploration a step further. By focusing your attention on a single point, such as your breath or a mantra, you cultivate a state of heightened awareness. In this state, you become a detached observer of your thoughts and emotions, watching them arise and dissipate like clouds in the sky. This ability to observe without judgment fosters self-acceptance and allows you to see your patterns and reactions with greater clarity. As you cultivate this inner awareness, the veil that separates you from your true essence begins to lift. This expansion of consciousness isn't just about intellectual understanding; it's a visceral experience of your interconnectedness with all things. The world around you comes alive with new vibrancy, and your perception of reality itself takes on a deeper and more meaningful dimension.

By incorporating these practices into your daily routine, you embark on a journey of self-discovery that elevates not just your physical well-being but also your energetic frequency and consciousness. You become a more present and aware participant in your life, and your connection to the universe around you strengthens. This newfound awareness empowers you to make choices that resonate with your authentic self and navigate the world with greater purpose and clarity.

Ayurvedic meditation incorporates some core principles but allows for some flexibility depending on your dosha. Here's a general guide to get you started:

Finding a Quiet Space:

- Create a comfortable and quiet space free from distractions. This could be a dedicated meditation room, a quiet corner of your bedroom, or even a serene spot outdoors.

Setting the Mood (Optional):

- You can enhance the ambiance with calming music or gentle scents like sandalwood or lavender (if not allergic).

Posture:

- Ayurveda recommends sitting in a comfortable, upright posture. You can sit on a meditation cushion on the floor, a chair with good back support, or even lie down (if you're new to meditation and prone to sleepiness). The key is to maintain a position where you can comfortably remain alert for the duration of your practice.

Breathwork (Pranayama):

- Many Ayurvedic meditations incorporate specific breathing techniques called Pranayama. A simple and effective technique for beginners is Dirga Swasham, also known as Three-Part Breath. Inhale slowly and deeply through your nose, filling your belly, then your chest, and finally your upper chest/clavicles. Exhale slowly and completely, reversing the order (upper chest, chest, belly).

Mantra or Focus Point:

- **Mantra Meditation:** Choose a mantra, a word or phrase that resonates with you. It could be a simple sound like "Om" or a Sanskrit mantra with deeper meaning like "Om Shanti" (peace). Silently repeat the mantra with each inhalation and exhalation. This repetition helps quiet the mind and creates a focal point for your attention.
- **Drishti Meditation (Gazing):** Select a fixed point to gaze at with a soft focus. This could be a candle flame, a specific spot on the wall, or even the tip of your nose. Don't strain your eyes; simply allow your gaze to rest gently on the chosen point.

The Practice:

- Begin with a few minutes of deep breathing exercises (3-5 minutes).
- Then, gently shift your focus to your chosen mantra or your breath.
- Inevitably, your mind will wander. Don't judge yourself; simply acknowledge the distraction and gently bring your attention back to your focus point.
- Start with shorter meditation sessions (5-10 minutes) and gradually increase the duration as you become more comfortable.

Tailoring to Your Dosha:

- **Vata Dosha:** If you're Vata dominant, focus on calming and grounding techniques. Try slow, deep breathing exercises and mantras with deeper tones like "Om."
- **Pitta Dosha:** For Pitta individuals, focus on cooling and pacifying practices. Use visualization techniques involving cooling colors like blue or white, and mantras with softer sounds like "Shanti."
- **Kapha Dosha:** If you're Kapha dominant, aim for stimulating and energizing meditations. Try shorter meditations with invigorating breathwork like Bhastrika (bellows breath) and mantras with brighter sounds like "Om Ram."

The key to success lies in consistent practice. Even a few minutes of daily meditation can yield significant benefits. Remember, mastering meditation takes time and patience. There's no one-size-fits-all approach; the focus is on cultivating a sense of inner peace and heightened awareness, however that unfolds uniquely for you.

Massage therapy also plays a vital role in the tapestry of Ayurvedic practices. Unlike a typical relaxation massage that focuses solely on muscle tension, Ayurvedic massage techniques delve deeper, aiming to influence the body's subtle energy channels known as marmas. Imagine these marmas as a network of energetic pathways coursing throughout your body, carrying the life force known as prana. When these marmas become congested or blocked, it can disrupt the flow of prana, leading to imbalances that manifest as physical discomfort, emotional distress, or even lowered vitality.

Ayurvedic massage therapists employ a variety of techniques specifically designed to clear these blockages and restore a smooth flow of prana. Depending on your specific needs and dosha, the therapist might use long, flowing strokes to stimulate sluggish circulation in a Vata dominant individual. For a Pitta dosha, gentler manipulations with cooling oils might be used to pacify excess heat and inflammation. Kapha imbalances might be addressed with more invigorating techniques to stimulate sluggish energy and eliminate toxins.

By addressing these energetic blockages, Ayurvedic massage promotes a more balanced flow of prana throughout your body. Imagine the feeling of a dam releasing, allowing the pent-up energy to course freely. This can manifest in a variety of ways, from a deep sense of physical ease and relaxation to a renewed sense of vitality. But the benefits extend beyond the physical. As prana flows more freely, it nourishes not just your body but also your energetic field. This can contribute to a heightened sense of well-being and a feeling of being more vibrantly alive. In essence, Ayurvedic massage helps elevate your energetic frequency, allowing you to experience a more radiant and conscious state of being.

In essence, Ayurveda offers a multifaceted approach to well-being. By combining a personalized diet with practices like yoga, meditation, and massage, you create a lifestyle that nourishes your body, mind, and spirit. This holistic approach is believed to not only promote physical health and prevent disease but also elevate your energy frequency and consciousness, fostering a sense of vibrant and expansive well-being that resonates on multiple levels.

Self Care and Releasing Negativity

In today's fast-paced world, self-care is no longer a luxury, but a necessity. It's the foundation for a healthy and fulfilling life. Yet, self-care goes beyond bubble baths and face masks. It also encompasses our emotional and energetic well-being. This is where vibrational healing practices come in. They offer a unique perspective on how our thoughts, emotions, and even physical sensations can vibrate at specific frequencies. When negativity takes hold, it can disrupt this energetic balance, lowering our vibrational frequency and impacting our overall well-being. Vibrational healing techniques aim to address these imbalances. By working with the body's energy field, they can help release negativity and promote a more harmonious state. This shift can have a profound effect, not only on our emotional state but also on our energy frequency and consciousness. As we release negativity and cultivate a more positive outlook, we elevate our energetic vibration, fostering a sense of well-being that resonates on multiple levels. In essence, vibrational healing empowers us to take charge of our self-care journey, promoting a life filled with greater peace, vitality, and a heightened sense of connection to ourselves and the world around us.

Your body is a complex instrument. When you nourish it with a healthy diet rich in whole foods, fruits, vegetables, and lean proteins, you are providing it with the building blocks for optimal performance. This not only translates to physical health but also energetic well-being. The high vibrational energy of these foods resonates within your system, promoting a sense of vitality and balance. Additionally, staying hydrated by drinking plenty of water throughout the day ensures a smooth flow of energy throughout your body. Think of water as a conductor, allowing energy to move freely and efficiently. When dehydrated, this flow can become sluggish, potentially contributing to a lower vibrational state.

Prioritizing quality sleep is essential for vibrational healing. It allows your body to recharge and restore itself on a deep cellular level. During sleep, your brain isn't simply idling; it's actively processing information, consolidating memories, and flushing out toxins. This restorative process translates to a more balanced energetic state when you wake up. Your body is like a battery – deep sleep is the recharge cycle. The more consistently you prioritize quality sleep, the fuller the energetic charge becomes in the morning.

A well-rested body is a body that vibrates at a higher frequency. Think of it like a musical instrument – a properly tuned instrument vibrates with a clear, harmonious sound. When you're sleep-deprived, your body becomes like a detuned instrument – the vibrations become sluggish and dissonant. This disharmony can manifest as fatigue, irritability, and a lower overall energy level. On the other hand, adequate sleep allows your body to fine-tune itself, promoting a sense of well-being and vitality. As your energetic state rises with better sleep, you'll naturally experience a more positive outlook and a greater capacity for joy. Remember, creating a consistent sleep schedule and establishing a relaxing bedtime routine are crucial for achieving quality sleep and promoting a higher vibrational state.

Moving your body is another wonderful tool for self-care and raising your vibrational frequency. Regular physical activity helps release endorphins, natural mood elevators, and promotes a sense of vitality. These positive emotions resonate at a higher frequency, lifting your overall energetic state. Find an exercise you enjoy, whether it's dancing, yoga, walking, or swimming. The key is to move your body in a way that feels good and brings you joy. This combination of physical movement and positive emotions creates a powerful synergy that can significantly elevate your vibration.

Immersing yourself in nature is a powerful tool for vibrational healing, offering a chance to cleanse and ground your energetic field. Imagine the natural world as a vast reservoir of pure, vibrant energy. Whether you take walks in the park, hike in the woods, or simply sit outside and breathe in the fresh air, you're connecting with this energy source. This connection allows nature's vibrancy to replenish your own, fostering a sense of renewal.

The exchange of energy that takes place in nature can be incredibly cleansing. As you connect with the natural world, it can help clear away negativity that may be clinging to your energetic field. Imagine stagnant energy dissipating, replaced by a sense of lightness and harmony. This shift within your energy field can contribute to a more positive emotional state and a heightened sense of well-being.

Spending time in nature isn't about strenuous activity or achieving a specific goal. It's about slowing down, quieting your mind, and allowing yourself to be present in the moment. The sound of birds singing, the feel of the sun on your skin, the scent of pine trees – these sensory experiences can all contribute to a sense of peace and groundedness. By allowing yourself to be present and receptive to nature's energy, you create space for your own energy to vibrate at a higher frequency, promoting a more positive and vibrant state of being.

Mindfulness practices like meditation are well known for their ability to cultivate inner peace and focus. By quieting the mind and observing your thoughts without judgment, you can begin to identify and release negativity. Think of your thoughts as energetic waves. Negative thoughts, like worry or anger, vibrate at a lower frequency. By acknowledging these thoughts and letting them go, you create space for more positive and higher-vibrational thoughts to emerge. This shift in your mental landscape can have a profound effect on your overall vibrational frequency.

Engaging in creative activities you enjoy also allows for self-expression and can be a powerful tool for releasing negativity. As you paint, write, dance, or explore any creative outlet that resonates with you, you tap into a wellspring of positive emotions and self-expression. These emotions, along with the act of creation itself, vibrate at a higher frequency. By expressing yourself creatively, you not only release negativity but also elevate your energetic state, fostering a sense of well-being that extends far beyond the physical realm.

Finally, a gratitude practice can significantly improve your mood and raise your vibration. Shifting your focus to what you're grateful for in life, big or small, brings your attention to the positive aspects of your existence. Gratitude is a powerful emotion that resonates at a high frequency. By taking time each day to reflect on the things you appreciate, you cultivate a more positive outlook and elevate your overall energetic state.

In essence, self-care practices are not simply about relaxation and indulgence. They are powerful tools for promoting vibrational healing. By nourishing your body, mind, and spirit through these practices, you can release negativity, elevate your energy frequency, and cultivate a sense of consciousness that is more connected, vibrant, and at peace.

Releasing negativity is also a crucial aspect of vibrational healing, paving the way for a higher energy frequency and a more expansive consciousness. Think of negativity as a heavy weight dragging down your energetic vibration. When you hold onto anger, resentment, or worry, these emotions act like energetic anchors, tethering you to a lower frequency. Releasing negativity allows you to shed these burdens and elevate your energetic state.

Journaling can be a great ally in vibrational healing, offering a safe space to release negativity and cultivate a higher vibrational state. Imagine your journal as a trusted confidant, a place where you can express your thoughts and feelings without fear of judgment. By putting pen to paper, you externalize these negative emotions, allowing them to lose their grip on you. The act of writing them down can be incredibly cathartic, like a cleansing rain washing away negativity.

Once you express these emotions on paper, a sense of release can wash over you. It's as if you've unburdened yourself of a heavy weight. This release creates space within you, allowing for more positive thoughts and emotions to emerge. As negativity dissipates, your energetic field can lighten and become more vibrant. This shift in vibration can contribute to a greater sense of well-being and a more positive outlook on life.

Journaling is a practice that can be tailored to your individual needs and preferences. You can write freely, letting your thoughts flow onto the page without editing or censorship. You can also use journaling prompts to explore specific challenges or emotions. The key is to find a method that resonates with you and allows for honest self-expression. As you consistently practice journaling and release negativity, you'll create a foundation for a higher vibrational state, promoting inner peace and attracting more positive experiences into your life.

Affirmations are another great way to counter negativity and reprogramming your subconscious mind. Our subconscious mind is constantly bombarded with messages, both positive and negative. Negative self-talk or limiting beliefs can take root there, influencing our thoughts and behaviors in unseen ways. Affirmations act as counter-messages, positive statements that we consciously repeat to ourselves. By choosing affirmations that resonate with you, such as "I am worthy" or "I am loved," and repeating them regularly, you can begin to overwrite those negative messages. Over time, these positive affirmations can become the dominant force in your subconscious, shaping your thoughts and emotions in a more positive way. This shift in your inner dialogue can have a profound effect on your energy frequency, promoting a sense of well-being and empowerment.

Forgiveness is an essential part of vibrational healing, often misunderstood as a gift bestowed upon someone else. In truth, it's a gift you give to yourself. Holding onto anger and resentment is like a self-inflicted punishment. It's akin to drinking poison hoping the other person will fall ill. These negative emotions become a heavy burden on your energetic field, creating a dense and stagnant energy that lowers your vibration.

The act of forgiveness, however, is not necessarily about condoning the other person's actions. It's about releasing yourself from the grip of negativity for your own peace of mind.

Imagine a balloon filled with dark, heavy smoke. Forgiveness is like letting go of the balloon, allowing the negativity to dissipate and lifting your energy to a lighter, more vibrant state.

By releasing negativity through forgiveness, you create space for positivity to flourish within you. This shift in your energetic field can raise your vibrational frequency, promoting a sense of well-being and inner peace. Remember, forgiveness is a journey, not a destination. There may be times when you need to revisit the process, and that's perfectly okay. Be patient with yourself and celebrate your progress along the way. The lighter and more vibrant your energy becomes, the more you'll attract positive experiences and elevate your consciousness.

Visualization is another way to influence your energy frequency and promote a sense of peace. Imagine yourself surrounded by a radiant white light, a symbol of pure and positive energy. As you visualize this light enveloping you, feel it cleansing away any negativity and filling you with a sense of calm and well-being. This visualization practice helps shift your focus from negativity to positivity, raising your energetic vibration and promoting a sense of inner peace.

The Emotional Freedom Technique (EFT) is another approach to releasing negativity. EFT involves tapping on specific acupressure points while focusing on the negative emotion you want to release. The tapping is believed to stimulate the body's energy meridians, helping to clear blockages and promote emotional release. Many people find EFT to be a helpful tool for managing stress, anxiety, and other negative emotions. By addressing these negative emotions, EFT can contribute to a more balanced and harmonious energetic state.

The key to Self Care techniques is to experiment and find what practices and techniques resonate most with you. There's no one-size-fits-all approach to releasing negativity. The most important thing is to be consistent with your practice. By incorporating these techniques into your daily routine, you can gradually clear away negativity, elevate your energy frequency, and cultivate a more expansive consciousness, fostering a sense of well-being that permeates every aspect of your being.

A Vibrant Conclusion

As you reach the culmination of this exploration, we hope you haven't simply finished a book, but embarked on a vibrant transformation. You've delved into the fascinating world of vibrational healing, uncovering a treasure trove of practices – sound therapy's calming waves, magnet therapy's invigorating pull, the ancient wisdom of chakra clearing and Ayurveda, the gentle touch of reiki, and the captivating world of crystals and aromatherapy. Each method offers a unique key to unlocking a higher energy frequency and an expanded consciousness.

Remember, vibrational healing isn't a rigid path with a single destination. The most transformative approach is the one that resonates most deeply with you. Perhaps the rhythmic vibrations of sound therapy resonated with your desire for inner peace, or maybe the vibrant energy of crystals sparked a sense of creativity. It's possible the time-tested wisdom of Ayurveda spoke to your holistic nature, or the gentle touch of reiki soothed your soul. The key lies in experimentation, embracing what resonates, and weaving a personalized practice that nourishes your well-being on physical, emotional, and spiritual levels.

This journey of raising your vibrational frequency isn't a finite act – it's a continuous exploration, an ongoing process of self-discovery and growth. As you integrate these techniques into your daily life, subtle shifts will likely emerge – a newfound sense of inner peace washing over you, a surge of creative energy propelling you forward, or a deeper connection blossoming between you and the world around you. These shifts are a testament to the rising frequency of your energy field.

Here are some final thoughts to illuminate your path forward:

Trust your intuition. It's your inner compass, guiding you towards practices that best suit your needs. When faced with a choice, quiet your mind and listen to the whispers of your soul. Intuition speaks in subtle nudges, a feeling of unexplainable drawnness to a particular technique or a sense of peace radiating from a specific crystal. By honoring these whispers, you allow your inner wisdom to guide you on your path to higher vibration.

Be patient. Raising your vibration is a journey, not a destination. Celebrate the small victories – a moment of mindful breathing, a gentle yoga stretch, or a heartfelt moment of gratitude. Trust the process, and know that consistent effort leads to profound transformation. Each mindful breath, each moment of self-compassion, and each act of self-care contributes to a gradual rise in your energetic frequency. Celebrate these small victories, for they are the stepping stones on your path to a more vibrant and expansive way of being.

Embrace self-compassion. There will be days when negativity creeps in, clouding your energy field. Forgive yourself, and with gentle kindness, guide your focus back to a positive state. Remember, self-compassion is the fertile ground from which self-love and a higher vibration can flourish. When you treat yourself with kindness and understanding, you create a safe space for healing and growth. This self-compassion allows your energy to rise naturally, fostering a sense of well-being that radiates outward.

Share your gifts. As your vibration rises, it naturally inspires those around you. Share your knowledge and experiences, becoming a beacon of light for others seeking their own path to higher consciousness. Remember, the energy of well-being is contagious, and by sharing your light, you contribute to a more harmonious world. As your own vibration rises, you become a source of inspiration for others, encouraging them to embark on their own journeys of self-discovery and healing. By sharing your gifts, you contribute to a ripple effect of positive energy, uplifting not only yourself but also the world around you.

You are a magnificent being of light and energy. By nurturing your physical body, calming your mind, and opening your heart, you elevate your vibration and create a life that resonates with joy, vitality, and a deep sense of connection to all that is. May your journey be filled with vibrant energy, expansive consciousness, and a profound sense of well-being that ripples outward, touching the lives of those around you.

Were you Inspired by the insights on vibrational healing? Share your thoughts and help others to elevate their energy and expand their consciousness!

Scan the QR code to leave a review for Vibrational Healing

Preview The New Book By

Sarah Ripley

Manifesting with Rituals, Spells, and Runes

Deep within us lies an innate power to shape our reality, a power harnessed by ancient pagans through rituals, spells, and the wisdom of nature. This book invites you to rediscover this magic, offering a practical guide to manifesting your heart's desires using timeless tools and techniques.

Step onto your path of magical creation with the foundational knowledge of establishing a sacred altar, your personal space for connecting with the unseen forces. Delve into the enchanting world of crystals, runes, and herbs, unlocking their unique properties and how they can amplify your intentions. Learn the language of the candles, letting their vibrant hues illuminate your desires and empower your rituals.

Harness the celestial rhythm of the moon, aligning your manifestations with the waxing and waning phases for optimal results. As you turn the pages, you'll encounter a wealth of powerful rituals and spells, designed to attract love, prosperity, healing, and more. Each practice is presented with clear instructions, making them accessible to both seasoned practitioners and curious beginners.

This book is not merely a collection of recipes; it's an invitation to embark on a personal journey of self-discovery and empowerment. As you engage with the practices within, you'll cultivate your intuition, refine your focus, and learn to harness the abundance of the universe. Remember, the most potent ingredient is your own belief, fueled by passion and purpose.

Whether you seek to nurture your creativity, attract abundance, or cultivate deeper self-love, this book serves as your guide, reminding you that the magic to manifest your desires lies within, waiting to be awakened. Let this journey empower you to rewrite your story, one intention, one ritual, one spell at a time.

About the Author

Sarah Ripley is a certified Life Coach, mentor, and author of books and journals on Numerology, Spirituality, Ancient Practices and Natural Healing. She is also a trained Chakra healer, Green Witch, and Master Herbalist.

Sarah has a passion for helping others to live their best lives. She believes that we all have the power to heal ourselves and create the life we want. Her work is focused on helping people to connect with their inner wisdom and intuition, and to develop the tools and skills they need to live their lives in alignment with their values and purpose.

Sarah has traveled throughout Asia, South America and Europe studying different cultures and spiritual beliefs. She is also a nature lover who has done extensive trekking in the Himalayas, Rockies and Andes Mountains. She is a passionate advocate for natural living and enjoys cooking with a completely natural diet. She spends her free time relaxing with her family and cats.

Sarah has been married for 28 years and has 2 adult children. She currently lives in Southeast Asia with her husband and 4 adopted street cats, where she continues to write, teach, and mentor others. She is also working on a new book about her experiences with natural healing and spirituality.